The Art of Uncertainty

The Art of Uncertainty

HOW TO LIVE IN THE MYSTERY OF LIFE
AND LOVE IT

DENNIS MERRITT JONES

JEREMY P. TARCHER/PENGUIN
a member of Penguin Group (USA) Inc.
New York

JEREMY P. TARCHER/PENGUIN
Published by the Penguin Group
Penguin Group (USA) Inc., 375 Hudson Street, New York, New York 10014, USA •
Penguin Group (Canada), 90 Eglinton Avenue East, Suite 700, Toronto, Ontario M4P 2Y3,
Canada (a division of Pearson Penguin Canada Inc.) • Penguin Books Ltd, 80 Strand,
London WC2R 0RL, England • Penguin Ireland, 25 St Stephen's Green, Dublin 2, Ireland
(a division of Penguin Books Ltd) • Penguin Group (Australia), 250 Camberwell Road,
Camberwell, Victoria 3124, Australia (a division of Pearson Australia Group Pty Ltd) •
Penguin Books India Pvt Ltd, 11 Community Centre, Panchsheel Park,
New Delhi–110 017, India • Penguin Group (NZ), 67 Apollo Drive, Rosedale,
North Shore 0632, New Zealand (a division of Pearson New Zealand Ltd) •
Penguin Books (South Africa) (Pty) Ltd, 24 Sturdee Avenue,
Rosebank, Johannesburg 2196, South Africa

Penguin Books Ltd, Registered Offices: 80 Strand, London WC2R 0RL, England

Most Tarcher/Penguin books are available at special quantity discounts for bulk purchase
for sales promotions, premiums, fund-raising, and educational needs. Special books
or book excerpts also can be created to fit specific needs. For details, write
Penguin Group (USA) Inc. Special Markets, 375 Hudson Street, New York, NY 10014.

Library of Congress Cataloging-in-Publication Data

Jones, Dennis Merritt.
The art of uncertainty : how to live in the mystery of life and love it / Dennis Merritt Jones.
p.   cm.
ISBN 978-1-58542-872-4
1. Uncertainty.   2. Life—Religious aspects.   I. Title.
BF463.U5J56   2011   2011006940
299'.93—dc22

Printed in the United States of America
7   9   10   8   6

Book design by Meighan Cavanaugh

This book is dedicated to the pioneers of every generation who, through either sheer inspiration or necessity, have made this world a better place by coming to the edge of uncertainty and leaning over that edge to unfold what is next. Whether pushed by pain or pulled by the infinite possibilities of a life worth living, they are proof that living in the mystery of that which is yet to be is not something to be feared, but something to which we can look forward. May their wisdom, faith, and courage to act be the legacy received by the next seven generations to come, knowing the best is yet to be.

Contents

Introduction

Have you ever read a good mystery novel that really had you wondering "who done it" until the very end of the book? Somehow the author kept you involved throughout the entire story by not giving you the answers you were seeking. In much the same way, life is also a mystery. The only difference is that when it comes to life, we often have a far greater attachment to knowing how the story is going to end long before it does, and we suffer greatly because of it.

Whether we are talking about our lives, our relationships, our careers, or any other aspect of our daily existence, most of us are greatly attached to knowing (controlling) in advance exactly how everything is going

to turn out. And, because of this, we live smaller, con-
densed, fearful little lives.

Life truly is the ultimate mystery: We are born from
the pure essence of divine creation, given a body in
which we rattle around for a given period of time, and
then we leave again, going back into the divine essence
from which we came. That, in and of itself, is amazing!
What a miracle . . . what a mystery! The space between
those two points is what we refer to as "life" and we
spend most of it trying to figure out why things are the
way they are and how we can manipulate, control, and
squeeze more out of it rather than living in awe of the
sweetness of the mystery itself.

—From *The Art of Being: 101 Ways
to Practice Purpose in Your Life*

On the day we are born we enter the Earth School, as my
friend Gary Zukav refers to it, not knowing a thing. The
soul may come overflowing with wisdom accumulated
along the eternal journey but the intellect is a blank slate.
As we mature, chronologically and emotionally, advanc-
ing in our understanding of the "rules" of living in a
human skin, the message we are given is that the more
we grow, the more we need to know. It is only through

this process that we can move forward in life. If our intention is to advance in our understanding of how to create a life worth living, it would be safe to say that one of the required courses in the Earth School curriculum is "The Art of Uncertainty." Learning how to live in the mystery of life, *and love it*, is the journey of a lifetime. And it can never begin too soon!

When my daughter was a toddler I read stories to her every night. Because of my desire to see her grow emotionally, mentally, and spiritually, I tried to read new books to her on a regular basis. She resisted, wanting always to hear the same story, *The Little Mouse, the Red Ripe Strawberry, and the Big Hungry Bear,* over and over and *over* again. One night, as I was reading the story to her, I got it: She wanted to stay with the same story because she knew how it would end. It was safe and comfortable for her to know in advance that the mouse did get the strawberry away from the big mean bear and managed to live happily ever after. Isn't that the kind of ending we all want to know awaits us in the story of our lives? For most of us this is a lifelong lesson.

Recently my wife, Diane, and I took our grandchildren, James and Cailin, to Disneyland for the simple pleasure of some "hang time" together. I was amazed at how the park had changed since I first visited it in 1958 as a kid. Beyond the staggering number of people, there are now many new rides that, shall we say, are a bit more intense than the ones I remembered. The last time I was at Disneyland, the most intense ride in the park was the Matterhorn, which by today's standard is a mild-mannered roller coaster. Compared to many of the newer rides, the Matterhorn rates right up there with the flying Dumbo ride.

Throughout the day, I found myself steering the grandkids to the rides I knew from fifty years ago, like the putt-putt cars at the Autopia and the Jungle Cruise. Of course, while they humored me by going on those rides with me (and they will *never* let me live that down), the grandkids were more intent on all the newer rides, which caused me to go a bit queasy just looking at them. One ride that I had not been on was Space Mountain, and I have to admit that it brought me to the edge of my comfort zone. As we were climbing into our "rocket ship" for the ride, I noticed the woman just getting out of our capsule stagger off in a daze and promptly proceed to lose her twenty-two-dollar Tomorrowland lunch. Suffice it to say that this didn't exactly push my "Oh, I am going to enjoy this ride because Disneyland *is* the happiest place in the world" button. Nonetheless, as uncertain as I was about what lay ahead on this radical speedball ride into total darkness, I strapped in and held on tight.

Trying something totally new by being willing to come to the edge of my own uncertainty and launching into the unknown really paid off. As it turned out, Space Mountain was, indeed, intense, loud, dark (very dark), and really juicy. By "juicy" I mean that, for an hour after the ride, I was enjoying an energetic endorphin rush (courtesy of God) that I would not have gotten had I stayed with the rides I already knew so well from the past. The awareness I had was that my Disneyland experience is very much a metaphor for our daily lives in many respects: I entered Disneyland that day projecting images from my own past experiences, expectations, and limitations onto my current experience, and this restricted my ability to freely enjoy the possibilities that lay just beyond the comfort zone of the known. To further elucidate the experience and awareness I gained that day, I offer a quote by Deepak Chopra who, in his usual display of elegant words and profound wisdom, makes this point very clear:

I have projected the same images day after day
Becoming prisoner to the known.
But the known is dead and past now
And I must buy my ticket to freedom
By embracing the fresh and unknown

We can continue to live in the restrictions of the life we have always known because it's safe and predictable. However, in so doing we become prisoners of the invisible jail of our own mind. Chopra is spot on: If we truly desire to experience the freedom to be the fully expressed beings we were sent here to be, we have no choice but to embrace the unknown; that is, the mystery of that which is yet to be. Let's face it, before anyone climbs on a wooden carousel horse, that person knows, from simple observation, where the merry-go-round is going to take him, which is round and round, in the same location—everything between where the ride begins and ends is in plain sight. Metaphorically speaking, there is nothing fresh and unknown about the merry-go-round. It's the same thing over and over again. Unfortunately, that's how many of us tend to live our lives. Our ride through life is far too often a projection of the same images day after day, and thus we become prisoners to the known. In the process, we also miss the "juice" that comes with the adventure of going where we have never gone before. We were sent here to be explorers—to push out, grow, and evolve. But this can only happen when we are willing to experience new rides in life.

If you are ready to set yourself free from your prison of sameness, read on. It may require you to step onto a new ride or two, leaving behind the comfort zone of the known. In the process you will come to the very edge of what you know, which is where the juicy mystery of uncertainty awaits you. Read this book with an open mind, and expect the unexpected, as if it's your first day at the amusement park called Planet Earth. You really are on the ride of your life, and you owe it to yourself to enjoy the mystery and the freedom it brings. After all, you have already paid admission!

Even at a young age, we begin to develop our attachment to the known, which always circles us back to a reference point called "the past." If we are honest with ourselves, we can see that for most of us this attachment to the known still finds a home in our adult consciousness or belief system. We all have some addiction to wanting to control the future, don't we? There is much comfort to be found in the confines of a box when we know where the edges are. But there is certainly no growth, no evolution, and no deepening of our spiritual nature within that box. There can also be no doubt that this attachment to the known is what keeps many of us from creating the life we truly desire. It's flat-out frightening to step into the unknown, yet that is where all new creation takes place. Throughout this book we shall be reminded in various ways that we cannot create anything new from within the field of what we already know. If we use only our past as a reference point for our future, we just create more of what we have already created, another version of the same thing. And today, more than ever, we know that much of what has worked in the past won't work anymore. No one knows what the future holds, nor should we. That would only dull the edge of our own evolution and diminish the desire to stay engaged in pursuing meaning and purpose, which is what makes life worth living.

Our consciousness is the filter through which the unlimited potential of the universe flows. It determines the size of the box we live in. If we want to create a larger life, we must expand the size of the box, that is, come to the edge and lean over. Ultimately, what we create in the future bears the imprint of what is embedded in our consciousness as possible today. It is nothing more than the Law of Cause and Effect at work. If we desire to create a new experience, we must introduce a new cause, and new causes will never be found in past experiences.

This reality creates a conundrum: To learn more, we have to be willing to leave the zone of the known and step into the void. Each time we advanced in school, from the first grade to the second grade, then to third, and all the way through high school, and perhaps college, we were required repeatedly to enter through doors to the unknown, trusting we would be provided with whatever we needed to learn to progress to the next level. It was a continual effort to expand the size of the box in which we had become comfortable. While there may have been some struggle and discomfort as we entered each new learning environment, we felt a great deal of satisfaction at the end of each school year, a sense that we had learned what we needed to learn and, more importantly, we were moving forward into the mystery of that which was yet to come with confidence.

Then things changed. As we matured into adulthood and acquired more material security and a position in life, we got quite comfortable in the relative known. This is also when "stuck-in-the-rutitis" can set in. Someone once defined a rut as a grave with no end. Many people end up living their entire adult life in the rut because they believe it's safe there. The risk of loss appears to be minimal as long as we keep our heads below the line of fire. No longer are Mom and Dad or the school system forcing us to step into the unknown. And it dawns on us that life might be much more risky than it was when we were children because it appears we have more to lose. So we settle in, and life on the merry-go-round begins. We know exactly where it is going . . . and that would be nowhere. This is when a part of us begins to wither and die. The rut is a grave; we just don't know it.

No matter how far we may or may not go in school, the analogy applies. The ultimate school is life itself.

From the day we are born—when we enter the mystery of not knowing—until the day we leave the planet, the only way to grow is to step into the unknown time after time. The basic reality is that there is no area of our lives where we are not *forced* to step onto the pathway of uncertainty at one point or another. This includes our relationships, careers, physical health, finances, and so on. Why not enter the mystery consciously and intentionally every day? Becoming friends with uncertainty is a wise thing. As we make living in the mystery a daily practice, we prepare ourselves for the adventure regardless of whether we are pushed onto the pathway of uncertainty by inspiration or desperation, or by pleasure or pain. In either case, we shall discover it is a journey we can learn to love. Consider *The Art of Uncertainty* a guidebook on how to step into the mystery of life and *love* it.

HOW TO USE THIS BOOK TO YOUR GREATEST ADVANTAGE

In *The Science of Mind*, Dr. Ernest Holmes wrote, "Realization, without application, is hallucination." We can have amazing insights and revelatory moments about life, but if we don't find a way to actualize what we realize, it is all for naught. You will find greater value in reading this book if you take the time to sit with the information and process it slowly, absorbing its deeper meaning and thinking about how it applies to you. There will be points throughout the book where I may suggest you return to a specific chapter to reread and reconsider what it means to you. I encourage you to take the time to do this because it will help reinforce cornerstone concepts vital to living with uncertainty and loving it. At the end of each chapter you will discover two tools to help you personalize and apply the ideas discussed in that chapter:

1. Points to Ponder & Personalize

In this section I summarize the essence of the chapter, highlighting the salient points that will help you determine how they might be relevant to your life. As you read this information, I encourage you to make an effort to personalize it—try to see where the ideas being presented may fit into your life in real time.

2. Mindfulness Practices

While it will be discussed more completely in chapter 14, suffice it to say that mindfulness is the practice of "remembering to remember," to be fully present in the current moment, no matter where you are or what you are doing, not thinking about yesterday or tomorrow. When you combine your spiritual beliefs with mindfulness, God, Infinite Presence, Universal Intelligence (or whatever name you may use to refer to your connection with Life), it becomes a present-moment experience, and that moment becomes sacred. As you do the Mindfulness Practices at the end of each chapter, you will discover that you won't be alone—the presence of the One will be right there with you as you step into the mystery of uncertainty.

Welcome to the journey.

To the Reader:
About the Word "God"

As you read this book, I encourage you to remember that words are simply symbols that represent beliefs, thoughts, and ideas. I am keenly aware that words frequently mean different things to different people. Throughout this book there are references to God. At times, however, I will use other words that mean the same thing to me and carry the same sacred vibration. For instance, depending on the context, I might use words such as The Source, The Infinite One, Being, He, She, Presence, Self, The Whole, Divine Mind, Life, The Beloved, Spirit, Universal Intelligence, and even It. Yet, in my mind and heart, I remain clear that these words refer to the One God, known by many different names, including many I have not mentioned here, and I respect them all.

We must each shape our relationship with God in a manner that makes It personal to us—that is what matters. In order for you to get the most out of this book, I invite you to move beyond any attachment to the words used and, instead, open your mind and heart to the meaning and intention behind them. This book is meant to help you to discover more of your authentic power, and its intention is to assist you in moving deeper within where, in wordless silence, you commune with Spirit, according to your own understanding of It.

Peace,
Dennis Merritt Jones

I.

COMING TO THE EDGE OF UNCERTAINTY

Pushed by Pain or Pulled by Possibilities

❦

Come to the edge, he said.
They said: We are afraid.
Come to the edge, he said.
They came.
He pushed them and they flew.

—GUILLAUME APOLLINAIRE

For the past few years my wife and I have been blessed to have the same family of sparrows return to a nesting spot they created on the ledge of the underside of our patio awning; it provides safety and shelter. We can see the nest from our kitchen window only ten feet away. While I have to admit they make quite a mess, it is a small price to pay for the privilege of watching the parents fortify the nest with sticks, weeds, feathers, and just about anything else they can find as they prepare to give birth to a new generation of winged master teachers. I refer to them as master teachers because, by witnessing them grow from helpless hatchlings to flying fledglings, I am reminded of what it means and what it requires to come to the edge of the unknown and lean into the mystery of life with abandon, which is also another word for detachment.

> In detachment lies the wisdom of uncertainty. . . . [I]n the wisdom of uncertainty lies the freedom from our past, from the known, which is the prison of past conditioning. And in our willingness to step into the unknown, the field of all possibilities, we surrender ourselves to the creative mind that orchestrates the dance of the universe.
>
> —DEEPAK CHOPRA

In the spring the mother laid four eggs, and it was a sacred experience to watch the babies grow. Finally the day came when they would be forced to leave the comfort and safety of the nest they had outgrown. One sunny day it was time for them to launch and take to the sky. The largest of the four chicks stepped out of the nest and onto the ledge for the first time, looking down at the ground some eight feet below. He stood perfectly still for a moment, as if sizing things up, and began to experiment with the awkward appendages we refer to as wings—stretching and flapping them so frenetically that he nearly fell off the ledge. He waddled several feet back and forth on the ledge, as if trying to decide whether he wanted to return to the nest or take the pending plunge. Then quickly, as if not wanting to give himself the opportunity to change his mind, he came to the edge and once again began wildly flapping his wings, intentionally leaning over until he reached the point of no return, simply surrendering to the pull of gravity. He instantly began to fly around under the patio awning, slowly widening his loop to extend to the grove behind the house. There he perched on the branch of an avocado tree, chirping his little heart out over his first successful experiment with life as a bird.

Then the second chick did the same as the first, followed by the third. But the fourth chick was a different story. The runt of the bunch, most likely because he was at the bottom of the pile, warily waddled to the edge of the ledge and looked down. Then he turned and briskly waddled back to the nest. There he sat for a good ten minutes trying to muster up the courage to follow his siblings. Hearing the festive chirping of his siblings in the grove must have been all the encouragement he needed. He bounced out of the nest, came running to the edge and, without even looking down, flapped his little wings wildly as he leaned over to a point where he had no choice—it was either fly or fall. Naturally, he flew, though he bumped into a few windows and walls before he made it out from underneath the awning and to the grove. When the family was complete, the birds flew several victory laps around the grove and were off to explore a world unknown to them before.

THE COURAGE TO BE WHO
YOU WERE BORN TO BE

It takes courage to grow up and become who you really are.

—E.E. Cummings

What can we learn about ourselves from my master teachers, the birds? By following the call of that ancient instinctual voice and falling into the unknown, they were on their way to becoming what they were born to be: full-fledged birds. It's the same as it has been for millennia. The only thing required for birds to soar to freedom beyond the confines of an enclosed little nest is the willingness to come to the edge of everything they have ever known and lean into the mystery. And so it is with us. In the words of John Maxwell, "If we're growing, we're always going to be out of our comfort zone." Just like the birds, we were born fully equipped to break free of past confining conditions that no longer serve us. And it is our destiny to do so. We were born to be free, to expand our horizons by going where we have never gone before, and not to hang out in the relative comfort and safety of the nest, the known. There is a place within us that is courageous beyond our human understanding; it yearns to explore beyond the boundaries of daily life. I know you can feel the same call to come to the edge that beckons me and every other person who has ever lived with passion, purpose, and meaning. Are we paying attention to that call, or are we resisting its nudge toward the edge?

Ernest Holmes referred to that inner impulse to push out as the "divine urge." It permeates every living thing, and its voice perpetually whispers in our inner ear, "Grow, grow, grow . . . I have to be more tomorrow than I was yesterday." But there is another voice that often speaks much louder, the voice of fear. It shouts, "No, no, no . . . stay, stay, stay! Stay right where you are because, while you may not like it, at least you know the rules and the boundaries. It is safe, and you risk nothing by staying put." Unfortunately, that is the big lie. There is *great* risk in resisting the divine urge to grow.

A UNIVERSAL IMPERATIVE:
GROW OR DIE

> It may be hard for an egg to turn into a bird: it would be a jolly sight harder for it to learn to fly while remaining an egg. We are like eggs at present. And you cannot go on indefinitely being just an ordinary, decent egg. We must be hatched or go bad.
>
> —C.S. LEWIS

It is a universal imperative that all living things must grow, and if they don't, they die. There is no middle ground. This universal imperative includes us. When we cease growing, a part of us begins to slowly die. This is inherently true physically, emotionally, and spiritually. When our body stops growing, it starts to wither. When our relationships stop growing, they begin to stagnate and die. The same is true for our careers, and everything else that needs the life force to sustain homeostasis, vibrancy, and health. Many people resist growth because it brings change, and change forces them into the mystery of the unknown.

LIKE IT OR NOT,
LIFE IS A MYSTERY

Those who insist on knowing the whys and hows of everything are not generally happy, healthy, and peaceful individuals. Their need to know is driven by fear and insecurity, not inspiration. The earthbound part of us cherishes the illusion that there is security in knowing what the future holds. Attachment to this illusion keeps us stuck in the zone of the known as we succumb to its voice of seeming logic and reason. That voice presents a compelling case for not ever taking the risk of leaving the nest of the known, and for avoiding change at all costs. The minute we yield to that voice and make the fear-based choice to settle for our current conditions, irrespective of how comfortable we are, an intangible but vital part of us begins to wither and die because its divine purpose is not being honored. That part of us is our soul. In *The Science of Mind,* Ernest Holmes states, "Nature will not let us stay in any one place too long. She will let us stay just long enough to gather the experience necessary to the unfolding and advancement of the soul. This is a wise provision, for should we stay there too long, we would become too set, too rigid, too inflexible. Nature demands change in order that we may advance."

Why do we resist the mystery that change brings? When we get too rigid and inflexible, rigor mortis of the soul sets in. For proof of this, we need look no further than to those who choose to stay in a relationship or job long after the soul, or life force, that originally brought it passion and joy has vacated the premises. The soul's nature is to evolve and push out, ever finding greater ways to express the Life we have been given. This expansion requires leaving the comfort of the known with the clear intention to continue learning, growing, exploring, and evolving. This takes not only courage, but curiosity and inquisitiveness as well.

CURIOSITY AND INQUISITIVENESS GETS US OUT OF THE BOX

> The important thing is not to stop questioning. Curiosity has its own reason for existing. . . . Never lose a holy curiosity.
>
> —ALBERT EINSTEIN

The key to our continued learning and personal evolution lies in the unknown, and curiosity and inquisitiveness unlock that door. Curiosity is the desire to learn about anything. It invites us to venture beyond the boundaries of what we already know; it compels us to step out of the box. Just watch any two-year-old child and you will see what I mean. Curiosity is energized by the spirit within that knows there is more to know. And the only way of learning what that is, is to follow its lead. I have a new master teacher by the name of Mac Doodle. He is a six-month-old Labradoodle/Goldendoodle mix. It doesn't matter what mission he is on, whether it's fetching the ball or just running wildly through the yard, he will often stop on a dime, turn, and begin intensely sniffing the scent of some "mysterious" creature, or chase an errant windblown leaf, or follow the sound of something into the bushes. His ability to be fearlessly curious about life in the moment seems to come naturally.

> Curiosity is lying in wait for every secret.
>
> —RALPH WALDO EMERSON

By the time Master Mac was four months old, he had explored every square inch of our back yard and was becoming a bit bored with it all. There were no more secrets, no more mysteries to solve. Then I took him on his first walk through the neighborhood, and he nearly went berserk with excitement. Every sense he had was

instantly alive with curiosity and wonder. He had entered a whole new level of learning in Classroom Earth
and, again, the quest to know more was on. The only difference between Mac and you and me is that, while he
can be curious, he can't be inquisitive. But we can. Inquisitiveness is the process of using our thinking mind,
inquiring or asking questions that allow us to clarify,
process, and absorb new information. It's a fast track to
learning. Just like Mac, our ability to be curious is innate.
We just have to access it and follow its lead. The good
news is that we can also ask questions along the way,
which enhances deeper learning. Be assured, we will be
asking many questions along the way as we journey together on the pathway of uncertainty. Like Mac, we
enter a whole new level of learning in Classroom Earth
every time we walk out the front door. We only need to
be open to exploring the wonder of it all. In the words
of Walt Disney, "We keep moving forward, opening new
doors, and doing new things, because we're curious and
curiosity keeps leading us down new paths." Amazing
things await you on the path just beyond the next door.
Pushed by pain or pulled by the possibilities, eventually
you will be compelled to pass through the door marked
"uncertainty." In either case, a great and wonderful adventure awaits you . . . so come to the edge, and breathe.

POINTS TO PONDER & PERSONALIZE

• Between a shaky world economy, increasing unemployment, and related issues, many today are being forced to come to the edge of uncertainty. Just like the baby sparrows, they find themselves leaning into the mystery that change brings, because they have no choice: It's fly or die. Others might be led to the edge because they have become aware of the divine creative urge stirring within, whispering, "There is more for you to know, to do, to be." What might be your motivation for coming to the edge of uncertainty?

• French novelist Anaïs Nin wrote, "There came a time when the risk to remain tight in the bud was more painful than the risk it took to blossom." What brings a person to the precipice of uncertainty varies. Sometimes it is the pain of desperation, sometimes the bliss of inspiration. In either case, if you are to unfold your true essence beyond the restrictions of a small, constrained existence, coming to the edge of all you know might look like a risk. But the universal imperative "grow or die" reminds us that *not* coming to the edge is an even greater risk and even more painful.

- Whether we come to the edge of uncertainty through inspiration or desperation, the principle remains the same. Within the baby sparrow there lies something that *knows* how to fly. It doesn't need to be taught; the knowing is inherent. Birds just have to be what they were born to be—birds. It is Infinite Intelligence working as instinct that flies the bird. Likewise, there dwells within you an Infinite Intelligence that *knows* how to support you, guide you, and sustain you. It is not something you need to learn, it's something you need to listen to, an inherent part of your being. Infinite Intelligence, working as intuition, accompanies you into the mystery. You just have to be willing to be who and what you were born to be. The promise is that you will be free to open new doors of self-discovery, and claim the resources to create a life worth living, if you are courageous enough to follow Its lead. Yes, action is required: Just like the fledgling birds, you must come to the edge of all you know, lean over, and open yourself to the amazing gift the mystery of life is offering you in every moment of every day, and then surrender to its gravitational pull, trusting you will be shown the way.

- The essential concepts in this chapter are choice, faith, curiosity, and action. The power to choose will be more fully examined in a subsequent chapter. But for now, suffice it to say that choosing to listen and having the faith to follow that guidance with action is a wise thing to do. Failure to do this has its consequences. A spiritual teacher, Shakti Gawain, wrote, "Every time you don't follow your inner guidance, you feel a loss of energy, loss of power, a sense of spiritual deadness." When you choose not to listen to and honor the guidance from within, you invite the universal imperative to have its way with you, and some of your life force begins to wane. Remember, curiosity and inquisitiveness are Spirit's invitation to get out of your box and explore the mystery of the unknown. Every action you take moves you one step closer to either evolution and expansion or redundancy and a reduction of your life force. The moment you make the decision either to act and grow, or not to act and thus to wither, the universe honors your choice in an impartial way. This makes choosing to come to the edge of uncertainty and leaning over a wise thing to do, doesn't it? What choice is calling you today, and what action will you take? Listen to your heart—you'll know. Then, get curious enough to open the door and take a peek. This is the first step in mastering the art of uncertainty.

MINDFULNESS PRACTICES

Dedicate some time today to exploring these questions, observing how you either welcome or resist examining your circumstances and beliefs about growth and uncertainty. This self-inquiry will reveal what is required for you to come to the edge consciously, trusting the process:

1. Clarify your motivation for stepping into the unknown. Are you seeking change today, or is change seeking you?

   • Are you being pulled to the edge of the unknown by possibilities, or pushed by pain? In either case, can you own it, knowing that the same principles for transcending any perceived limitations apply to both?

   • Acknowledging what brings you to the edge is the first step. Dedicate time today to consciously embracing the idea that you are willing to come to the edge of uncertainty and lean over just a bit, and breathe. How does that *feel*?

2. There are many ways people justify remaining in a rut. Sometimes they resist growing beyond their cur-

rent situation because they fear the disapproval of others, or they lack the skills needed, or they might be forced to stretch.

- How and why have you been avoiding coming to the edge of the unknown? Take a few minutes and journal about whatever comes to mind. Don't judge it, just acknowledge it.
- Seek out someone you trust who may have already stepped into the same mystery of the unknown that is calling you. That person will be easy to spot because he or she is already doing what you are being called to do. Invite that person to mentor you and be your cheerleader, just as the sibling sparrows encouraged the last chick to fly from the nest, knowing if they can do it, so can you.

3. After considering these questions and practices, what action are you willing to initiate that will move you toward the mystery of uncertainty? Remember, for the willing, anything is possible. But you have a role to play. It's true that God feeds the sparrows, but He doesn't drop the worms into their beaks.

- Make curiosity part of your daily practice. Do some self-inquiry and ask questions that cause you to

stretch for the answers. Then take that sense of curiosity with you into your daily life. Explore, ask
questions, be open to whatever shows up, and learn
from it.

- Make a list of at least three actions you can initiate
today, and keep it in front of you as a reminder of
the choices you get to make. The universe awaits a
sign from you. *Come to the edge . . .*

2

THE ANATOMY OF FEAR

Dancing with Your Demons

Driven by fear, people run for security to mountains
and forests, to sacred spots and shrines. But none of
these can be a safe refuge, because they cannot free
the mind from fear.

—THE DHAMMAPADA

As we begin our sojourn into the mystery of uncertainty we will be reminded rather quickly that nothing triggers fear of the unknown faster than that which we cannot see—our minds do a marvelous job of running ahead of us in the apparent darkness, creating all sorts of scary diversions and reasons for not moving forward. I vividly remember, as a ten-year-old boy, walking home alone many nights from my friend Tim's after dark. When I say "walking," I have to chuckle because seldom did I walk; I ran like my pants were on fire. This was my first memorable experience of what it really meant to travel the path of uncertainty by myself, and it frightened me immensely. I had to traverse through a deep, half-mile long ravine that ran all the way from the back of his house to mine. It was pitch-dark and there were numerous critters (some real and many imagined, I am sure), noises, and countless holes and fallen trees around which I had to navigate. This was not an easy thing to do in total darkness, and yet somehow I always managed to make it home unscathed. The problem was that each time I had to run the gauntlet again, there were those same fears, waiting for the race to begin. Over the years I outgrew running through ravines in the dark, but some of those fears continued to chase me all the way into adulthood as I traveled new pathways that were necessary to my creating a life worth living. It was years before I made peace with the reality that the fears I frequently wrestled with had taken up permanent residence in my mind, and that only I could evict them.

LOOKING THE BEAST IN THE EYES

> What is needed, rather than running away or con-
> trolling or suppressing or any other resistance, is un-
> derstanding fear; that means watch it, learn about it,
> come into contact with it. We are to learn about fear,
> not how to escape it.
>
> —JIDDU KRISHNAMURTI

Are you aware of this acronym for F.E.A.R: **F**alse **E**vi-
dence **A**ppearing **R**eal. I have another one for you: **F**orget **E**verything **A**nd **R**un. Isn't that what we often do
when a fear thought appears in our mind, triggering our
emotions? We reactively turn from the fear and run away
as fast as we can. In the East it is said that we must learn
to dance with our fear because the closer we can get to
it, the more fully we can make peace with it. In her
book, *When Things Fall Apart*, Pema Chodron writes,
"No one ever tells us to stop running from fear. We are
very rarely told to move closer, just to be there, to become familiar with fear. . . . But the advice we usually
get is to sweeten it up, smooth it over, take a pill, or
distract ourselves, but by all means make it go away."
The practice is to understand it's not about slaying the
monster; it's about learning to lead the dance. If we are

to ever master the art of living peacefully, purposefully, creatively, courageously, and joyfully in the midst of uncertainty, there is no question that fear is the boogeyman we have to face first. This requires us to dance cheek-to-cheek with our demons rather than run from them. If we are willing to listen, fear can be a great messenger to get our attention, and can even serve us well in certain circumstances. However, it's vital to remember that fear has no life of its own, other than that which we choose to give it. Fear is a word (or label) to which we have learned to assign certain emotions. Getting comfortable with our fear means taking the time to stand face-to-face with it and understanding why it is there, even if it frightens us in the process.

In my early adult years, when I was still naive enough to believe I could outrun my fears, I used nearly every possible means to avoid facing them. Sometimes I would run from my fear by turning to recreational drugs, substances such as alcohol and food, or by engaging in casual sex, or going shopping for the latest guitar (you should have seen my guitar collection) and other such diversions. I actually had different avoidance strategies depending on which "fear du jour" I was trying to evade. The problem was that none of those diversions ever slew the monster of fear; they only diverted my mind from fear's presence for a brief time. When I came back from my trip on the "river of denial," my fear was waiting there for me like a loyal pet. Can you relate?

> When fear ceases to scare you, it cannot stay.
>
> —GARY ZUKAV

What we really need to do, rather than run from our fear, is run *toward* our fear and meet it head-on. Wisdom says that the better we understand something, the more logically we will be able to deal with it. We might best understand the anatomy of fear by first dissecting it and seeing it for what it is *and* what it is not. By understanding the nature and origin of fear, we will be less frightened by it and far more able to live with it in the "hallway (or, in my case, ravine) of uncertainty." The "hallway of uncertainty" is often that dark and lonely place between where we have been and where we are going.

When I say that we must learn how to live *with* fear, it doesn't mean living life in a fearful way. Rather, it means living life in spite of fear, understanding that as long as we are in a human skin, fear will be popping up from time to time. It's a standard operating program that comes pre-installed as part of the package called "being alive." All of God's creatures have been imbued with this survival tool, so we may as well get used to the idea that we are hardwired to experience fear as part of our inherent, primal, self-survival programming; and that's a good thing. Without some fear we would probably not make it to our adult years.

> The problem is that, somewhere along the way, the line between what to fear and what not to fear has been blurred.
>
> —DMJ

WHERE DOES FEAR ORIGINATE?

At first, it might appear that fear comes *from* the very thing we are fearing, be it a threat of physical harm, a scary prognosis from a doctor, a crashing stock market, and so on. The reality is that fear can't come from outside of us. Fear is a feeling that wells up inside us as a *reaction* to an outer stimulus. That stimulus can, and does, change constantly. But it is generally attached to a concern about the loss of something in our world of people, places, and things, such as a job, a lifestyle, a relationship, a reputation, a title, or a material possession. It might even be a fear of the ultimate loss: A loss of the life of a loved one or even our own life. In short, our underlying, and most often unseen, fear is triggered by undesired change of any kind. Change can push us out onto the ledge of uncertainty with all its terrifying ramifications. As we'll discover in the next chapter, change is really the only constant in life, so we must learn to welcome it if we want to create a life worth living.

As awakened, evolving human beings, we begin to realize it is our choice whether we shall mindlessly *react* to fear or mindfully *respond* to fear. How we consciously perceive fear will determine our ability to step into the unknown with clarity and confidence. This requires us to be emotionally aware and willing to stand face-to-face with "what is," and examine what we see and feel and, often, what we *don't* see and feel. In the metaphysical writings of *A Course in Miracles,* a passage states, "You only have two emotions, love and fear." In other words, if we are not experiencing authentic love, fear is somehow making a guest appearance. If this is the case, becoming emotionally aware is a prerequisite for being able to identify our fear with all of its convincing disguises that, on the surface, don't always look or feel like fear. At times, fear dresses up in its Sunday best and reveals itself as worry, doubt, concern, and other "well-meaning" emotions. At other times, fear insidiously lurks behind the scary mask of anger, the obsessive mask of jealousy, the green mask of envy, the toxic mask of resentment, and other such highly charged emotions. Becoming mindful of our emotions is paramount to understanding the role that fear plays in our life.

THE ILLUSION OF CONTROL

> The closest to being in control we will ever be is in
> that moment that we realize we're not.
>
> —BRIAN KESSLER

Often fear originates in our mind because, try as we may,
we have little control over the future. And the future
is where we tend to look for our security, seeking the
assurance that everything will be all right. The illusion
is that we have control over many variables in our daily
life and that seems to make us feel better, at least temporarily. However, we really have control over very little,
other than our next breath and our next thought. Consider these questions: Can you control the driver in the
next lane? Can you control the surges of the waves in
the ocean? Can you control the earth when it quakes?
Can you control the stock market and the direction of
the world economy? Can you control the weather? Can
you control the jumbo jet in which you are a passenger?
Can you control your spouse/partner/parents/children's
behavior or actions? Can you control the natural aging
process of your physical body? Can you control the fact
that one day you and those you love will no longer be
on the planet? The obvious answer to all of these ques-

tions is the same, yet look at how much time, energy, and power we expend trying to do so.

The only thing we have control over is our choice to either *react* mindlessly or *respond* mindfully to "what is" in the current moment. There it is: To practice the art of uncertainty is to get comfortable with being "out of control." By this, I don't mean being out of control of our own actions and behavior, but rather letting go of the need to control the actions and behavior of other people, including their opinions of us. It also means understanding that we have no control over the future, what "should or shouldn't" happen tomorrow, but at the same time, it means developing an inner knowing that everything *will* be all right.

> Who is more foolish, the child afraid of the dark or the man afraid of the light?
>
> —MAURICE FREEHILL

Sometimes we avoid seeing the truth that lies behind our fear because then we'll have to deal with that reality. However, there is something very empowering about turning and facing our fear and shedding new light on it. Once exposed to the light, the things we fear seem to lose their power to scare us. Someone once said, "Fear is the little darkroom where negatives are developed." As we drag our fear out of the darkened recesses of our mind and into the light of day through courageous self-inquiry and logical, spiritually grounded thinking, the energy that we have given to what we fear begins to diminish right before our eyes. Think of Infinite Presence as Light, or that which is indestructible, right there in the midst of our darkest fears. In the Bhagavad Gita it is written, "Fear not what is not real, never was and never will be. What is real always was and cannot be destroyed." Life is real, Light is real and can never be destroyed; all else comes from the shadow world of our own imagined separation from that which is real. As we call forth the awareness of Infinite Presence as our sole/soul Source, shedding Its radiant light on our fear, we in turn take back the power we have bestowed on that fear. When fear ceases to scare us, we can then watch it disappear into the nothingness from which it came.

POINTS TO PONDER & PERSONALIZE

• While your story may be different from mine, can you trace your fears back to their points of origin, any of the fears that may be showing up in your life today? If you think about the fears you had as a child, can you see how they may have morphed into your adult life and taken on a new role? As an example, I don't run from things I can't see in the dark anymore, but life continues to present scary dramas and fear pops up its head from seemingly nowhere. When that happens, I still get that initial intense chill factor I so vividly remember as a boy. The only difference now is I don't react to what I can't see because I know the fear is within me, not "out there." If you can locate one (or more) of those fears, notice how much of its power to sustain itself is being drawn from what you *can't* see.

- Considering the acronym for FEAR—**F**orget **E**verything **A**nd **R**un—in what ways might you be avoiding your fears, rather than facing them? This can be a difficult question with which to conduct self-inquiry; however, it is the first step to getting onto the dance floor with your fear where you can learn to lead the dance. The key is to become the observer of your actions and thoughts, and then challenge your beliefs behind them. Do you tend to turn toward the use of substances or behaviors that temporarily divert your attention from whatever the stimulus of your fears may be? As you become witness to the manner in which you avoid your fears, you can then make a choice to challenge them by consciously responding to them rather than reacting and running from them. One of the few things you have even a modicum of control over is your ability to choose to "respond" rather than "react" to whatever is stimulating the fear within you. To respond mindfully, rather than react mindlessly, you must be conscious, emotionally aware, and dialed into the present moment, which is where your true point of power exists.

• It is important to understand that underneath all emotions, including fear, lies the authentic Self patiently awaiting our awakening to its presence. The question worth exploring is: How do we access and live from the authentic Self? Think of several of the people you admire and consider to have lived authentically empowered lives. By this I mean those you see as being "real"—those who developed the ability to be who they really are, 24/7. These people can be historical figures or people who are currently living—you might even know them personally. (A few who would be on my list would be Jesus, Gandhi, Mother Teresa, and Martin Luther King, Jr.) From your list, notice that the one common element in every person you chose is that they lived life fearlessly. This is not to say they didn't have the same challenges we have, which causes fear to rise from within; they simply were not willing to let that fear define who they knew themselves to be. These are the truly free and liberated people of the world. The authentic Self knows no fear because Its point of origin is Infinite Presence, which is Love in its highest vibration. Seek to deepen your relationship with your authentic Self.

• Socrates wrote, "The unexamined life is not worth living." When you enter into self-inquiry, you start to get answers that make life worth living, in spite of your deepest fears. With conscious, present-moment, emotional awareness comes the ability to identify and challenge your fear—to literally lift off the mask behind which your fear has been hiding. When you are conscious and willing to dance with your fear, it can become your teacher. This does not mean it leads the dance. It means that, if you are teachable, your fear will give you needed information to transform your moments of uncertainty into growth opportunities and healing. By realizing that your fear arises from within you, and not in the world, you can gain great understanding about yourself and life.

MINDFULNESS PRACTICE

This practice invites you to set aside some quiet time for introspection and self-inquiry. Create an environment that is private and, most of all, one that feels safe. Mindfulness means being present in the moment with "what is," and allowing it to be not only your experience, but also your teacher. Have a pen and paper handy because you may want to take some notes regarding the conversation you are going to have with your fear.

1. After a brief time of quiet mindful breathing, deepening your awareness of Infinite Presence, invite your fears to step out of the dark corners of your mind and into the light.

   • Some fears that appear will be expected because they have been lifelong companions, but don't be surprised if some unexpected fears reveal themselves as well.

   • Remember, many fears linger behind the masks of the emotions you may have never before identified as fear, such as anger, resentment, jealousy, despair, a need to control, a lack of control, and so on.

   • One at a time, look into the eyes of each fear and

ask, "What message do you bring me regarding my
attachment to this issue at hand that has so much
negative energy wrapped around it?" Don't debate
or argue with what is revealed, just listen and take
notes and then thank it for the gift it has given you.

- Remembering that fear is about a concern of loss of
someone or something, including control of people, events, and things, ask the all-knowing Infinite Intelligence within, "What lesson do I need to
know about what this fear has revealed to me surrounding uncertainty and loss, so that I may be at
peace in this moment with 'what is'?" Breathe, listen, and breathe some more, knowing this is the
act of shedding light on the darkness.

2. Understand that mastering the art of uncertainty does
not mean you will never experience fear; it means
you know how to lead the dance. It also means that
you are comfortable enough with "not knowing" to
still move forward, creating a life worth living. Ultimately, it means you have chosen to not allow fear to
keep you from fully *living* in the mystery of life and
loving it.

3.

LIKE IT OR NOT,
THIS TOO SHALL PASS

The Good News and the Other News

The Buddha taught that everything is impermanent—flowers, tables, mountains, political regimes,
bodies, feelings, perceptions, mental formations, and
consciousness. We cannot find anything that is not
impermanent. . . . We think that impermanence
makes us suffer. It is not impermanence that makes
us suffer. What makes us suffer is wanting things to
be permanent when they are not.

—THICH NHAT HANH

All changes, even the most longed for, have their
melancholy; for what we leave behind us is a part of
ourselves; we must die to one life before we can enter
another.

—ANATOLE FRANCE

I recall years ago how I wept when my dog needed to be put down because he had reached that point in his life where his pain was greater than he could bear. It was like losing my very best friend, and letting him go was among the most difficult things I have ever had to do. I also remember, at the tender age of thirteen, when my first girlfriend dumped me. Oh, the pain and indignation of it all. I pined and whined over her for what seemed an eternity. Then, there was the time in college when I needed to part with my favorite guitar because the rent was late. That hurt more than a root canal. In addition, deeply etched in the walls of my mind and heart is the memory of the grieving process I went through when my daughter was no longer my little girl, but growing into a young woman. Those special "daddy and daughter days" were gone forever. On the other hand, I also remember the years I felt trapped in a relationship and a career where the joy, passion, and love for both had died long before they actually ended. I couldn't get out of either fast enough, but for various reasons they just went on and on. In short, throughout my life when undesired change happened and I resisted it, or when desired change *didn't* happen when I wanted it to, I suffered. This is not just my story, it's the story of all humankind.

Can you recall the times in your life when you suffered

the most? Regardless of when or where it was, the likelihood is that the suffering was attached to your desire to have something in your life stay the same when, in actuality, it was in the "process" of changing, or you were attached to wanting something to change *before* it was ready to. Most likely it was an issue concerning your (or someone else's) relationship, health, material possessions, career, or financial status. In essence someone, something, or some condition was either coming or going when the preference was to keep things just the way they were, or else they weren't coming or going fast enough.

Change happens. Depending on your perspective—which will be determined by the level of your consciousness and your sense of unity with life or separateness from life—that's either the good news or the bad news. Uncertainty and change go hand in hand. Whether you like it or not, change happens when it is ready to. It is an inevitable and necessary part of your experience on this planet, and with change often comes the uncertainty of when it will happen and where it will take you. There is great wisdom in the ancient saying, "This too shall pass." It confirms that you can and should expect change and uncertainty as a natural part of your life experience because nothing (and no thing) lasts forever. The sooner you learn this life lesson, the less you shall suffer. Mastering the art of uncertainty will enable you to approach change with nonattachment (or at least less attachment), and in the process, the portal through which change can flow will open with grace and ease.

> If you're in a bad situation, don't worry—it'll change.
> If you're in a good situation, don't worry—it'll change!
>
> —JOHN A. SIMONE, SR.

If you are like most people, your tendency is to resist change and grasp the status quo because it's familiar and therefore comfortable, or to push for change before its time has come because you are uncomfortable with "what is." In either case, the irony is that change is the only constant and it is coming whether you want it to or not. This could be referred to as the Law of Impermanence because it is a universal principle that everything that has a beginning must have an end. This includes the moon and stars above and the earth below, the flowers in your garden, your beautiful looks, your car, your home, your bank account, your job, every positive and negative emotion you have, every relationship you have, everything in which you find pleasure or pain, as well as the physical body in which your soul essence is currently navigating the planet; it all has an expiration date. It is when we either resist or try to force the Law of Impermanence that we suffer.

The one exception to the Law of Impermanence is the principle of Life itself, which is greater than the form it occupies. I use the word "Life" in the context of another name for Infinite Intelligence or Cosmic Energy. Life is indestructible because it is the eternal divine essence of Infinite Intelligence before, during, and after it manifests as form. The energy that Life is never changes; only the form in which it temporarily manifests changes. It's our attachment to the ever-changing forms that causes our suffering. Perspective really is everything.

> That nothing is static or fixed, that all is fleeting and impermanent, is the first mark of existence. It is the ordinary state of affairs. Everything is in process. Everything . . . is always changing, moment to moment.
>
> —PEMA CHODRON

As we learn to change our perspective of things by witnessing that everything is "in process," we can transform our suffering into a deeper understanding that all of Life is simply a river that flows on and on eternally. We can wade out into the river and resist the current for a short span of time (known as our lifetime), or we can surrender to it and let go, trusting that the current knows what it's doing and where it's going. There is an old Indian saying that goes, "One can never stand in the same river twice." The reason is that the river is not the river-bed; it is the water that flows through the riverbed, and it is always flowing forward. Water is the spiritual symbol for Life. To resist the river's current is to resist the forward movement of Life, which is to choose suffering. On the other hand, to try to force change before it is ready is like trying to push the river faster than its natural flow.

So what does it require for us to transcend our resistance to or need to push the current, and to literally let go and surrender in our uncertainty to the flow of Life that absolutely knows what it is doing and where it is going? This is where having faith in our unity with something larger than ourselves can alter our perspective of how change operates in our lives.

EMBRACING CHANGE REQUIRES DEEP FAITH, BUT FAITH IN WHAT?

> Faith is the substance of things hoped for, the evidence of things not seen.
>
> —HEBREWS 11:1

What does faith mean to you? My dictionary defines faith as confidence or trust in a person or thing, or a belief that is not based on proof. Considering the above quote from the scriptures, faith is an inner knowing that does not rely on the outer world to verify or validate that knowing. The real question is, in what or whom do you have faith and, perhaps the larger question is, how? How do you experience faith? That is the juicy thing about faith; the "how" is often indescribable because it is unique to every human being. Because it is an inner knowing and, to many a feeling, we can't really point at faith and say, "There it is." However, we can point to the things that inspire our faith.

> Faith is daring the soul to go beyond what the eyes can see.
>
> —WILLIAM NEWTON CLARKE

When we study the anatomy of faith from a spiritual perspective, we discover that faith is the inner link to a universal Presence that goes beyond all form. Some might look to a particular spiritual or religious icon to deepen their sense of faith in what they can't see with the human eye, while others may be inspired to a deeper faith simply by gazing into the mystery of life found in a newborn baby's eyes or, for that matter, even a flower or a beautiful sunset. No matter what may be the inspiration, faith is an inner knowing that we are connected to something omniscient, omnipotent and omnipresent— something infinitely larger than ourselves that knows what It is doing. This depth of faith brings a sense of well-being, comfort, and inner peace to us in a world filled with so much fear and uncertainty. In short, it helps us surrender to and trust the process of change.

> I surrender my body to be ruled by my Mind;
> I surrender my mind to be governed by my Soul;
> and I surrender my Soul to the guidance of God.
>
> —WALLACE T. WATTLES

Rabindranath Tagore wrote, "Faith is a bird that feels dawn breaking and sings while it is still dark." Having faith in our unity with a Higher Power brings with it an unspoken expectation that our good lies before us, even in the midst of our darkest moments of uncertainty. There are as many names for this Higher Power as there are religions. While "God" is a universally used and accepted name (label), regardless of which spiritual tradition and path we walk or what we may choose to call that Higher Power, as we spiritually evolve, we naturally deepen our faith in our connection with It. Even our worst fears can be mitigated by our awareness of our oneness with the source of all life, all good. If this is true, then what's to resist or push when it comes to the inevitable changes that being alive brings? At first this may sound a bit spiritually cavalier. However, a deeper look into the truth of it will bring an unfathomable sense of inner peace.

> God, grant me the serenity to accept the things
> I cannot change, the courage to change the things
> I can, and the wisdom to know the difference.
>
> —REINHOLD NIEBUHR

As we spiritually mature, we begin to understand that faith in the unseen presence of the Infinite One is not so much about having that presence magically fix the problems in our life, as much as it is helping us embrace the "what is" that accompanies most change, knowing we are not dealing with it alone. When we enter each day with faith that we are connected with a presence and power that is larger than us, it seems easier to trust life and surrender to what is, in the moment. That doesn't mean we will always like what that moment brings, but with faith we are able to trust the process and find peace in the moment of what is.

LEARNING TO TRUST THE
PROCESS *IS* A PROCESS

The unfolding of life itself is a process, a sacred contin-uum where every "now" moment seamlessly connects with the moment just before and just after it. In other words, both the past and the future connect in the pres-ent moment and, if you are interested in accessing them, both have information for you regarding the change and uncertainty you may currently be facing. That infor-mation will affirm why you can have faith in the pres-ent moment, even in the midst of what is. If we are not mindful, it is very easy to allow the drama(s) in the mo-ment to distort the long view of life.

Try this visualization: Regardless of what may be going on in your life today, in your mind's eye, go back ten years. Get in touch with where you were spiritually and emotionally, and imagine that you could send your current self back to that space in time, taking with you what you *now* know about life. Just take a few minutes to realize how far you have come. Think about how much you have learned, grown, and changed. In other words, consider how much you have evolved in the past ten years, surviving all the changes and challenges that back then may have seemed unfathomable.

Do this process again, only this time, set your "time machine" for thirty years or, if you are old enough, fifty years ago. Now, imagine what wisdom you might impart to the "old you." If you could somehow magically do this, the likelihood is that you would probably be able to circumvent some of the pain and difficulties you went through on your journey. However, the larger question is whether you would really want to change any of your experiences on the journey, even if you could. The likelihood is that whatever it is that you have gone through and grown through has assisted you in becoming who you are today. This awareness alone should build your faith in the present moment.

Now for the second part of this visualization: This time go forward. Regardless of what may be going on in your life today, and given your current intention to grow and evolve, imagine where you might be spiritually, emotionally, and materially, twenty or thirty years from now. Yes, you may be going through something that is challenging you today but, remember, it is precisely those challenges that are currently offering you the "growth opportunities" that will assist you in becoming who you will be ten, twenty, or thirty years from now. It's the same cycle and process that brought you to "now" from twenty, thirty, or fifty years ago. Again, perspective is everything.

It can be easy to feel overwhelmed by the immensity of what may be looming directly in front of you, and that's when it may help to remember this visualization. In those moments when you might feel most uncertain, lost, isolated, or fearful of the unknown, imagine standing right next to you is the "future you" who already knows the truth, smiling because he or she understands that the burdens, changes, and uncertainties of the moment are also the blessings that will help you become who you have come here to be.

Trust founded in the faith of our oneness with the continuum of Life is the key to surrendering, with abandon, to what this moment and every moment brings, knowing "this too shall pass."

POINTS TO PONDER & PERSONALIZE

- Are you excessively attached to a person, circumstance, condition, or thing that is "in process" of either coming or going in your life? If so, is that attachment causing you pain? Perhaps it is regarding the death or loss of someone or something near and dear to you. It may be a concern regarding a change in your physical body either due to health or age, or a change of family dynamics due to divorce or the empty-nest syndrome, or perhaps it has to do with a career or lifestyle ending unexpectedly, and so on.

- Likewise, are you suffering from any attachment to a change you desire to have happen *before* it is ready to happen in its own natural space and time? These are all legitimate, real-life issues that, when considered, comprise the elements that make life worth living. You can find great comfort in the wisdom of knowing and affirming daily that regardless of the change at hand, this too shall pass. The Law of Impermanence guarantees this is true. The practice is to be highly involved in the "process" of witnessing the change, while at the same time knowing you don't have to be attached to the outcome because it's part of the natural process of life. In the metaphor of the river, this means wading in and trusting that the infinite flow of Life knows better than you where it is going. Yours is to surrender to the flow and trust the process. This concept will be more fully examined in the next chapter.

- In these challenging times, crises seem to be everywhere. If you are willing to look, you can know that in every crisis lies an opportunity. Each crisis you have is the universe's way of manifesting (in a way you can't avoid) the dynamics that facilitate a change that is inevitable. If you are conscious, a personal crisis invites you to examine old habits and your attachments to the way things have been that have kept you stuck. In the process, you can choose to introduce a new way of thinking about the change that lies before you. I have heard it said that in Chinese the symbol for crisis also means "opportunity." Whatever crisis you might be faced with, can you see how the Law of Impermanence, however painful in the moment, can also be an opportunity and a blessing to you?

- Can you see that each time the dynamic of change appears it is an invitation to dive more deeply into your faith? What role does faith play in "trusting" the process when it comes to managing change in your daily life? Do you tend to wait until there is a crisis at hand before you summon your faith, or is it something you practice with regularity? This is why it is wise to dedicate time daily to developing a relationship with that which you consider to be your Higher Power. Metaphorically speaking, it is much easier to find a fire extinguisher when there is a fire to put out if you instinctively know where the extinguisher is *before* you have the emergency. What practices could you commit to doing daily that would assist you in deepening your faith? Meditation is a powerful way to experience your unity with life. Through self-inquiry, explore what faith really means to you and how you can practice it every day.

MINDFULNESS PRACTICES

If we are to master the art of uncertainty, we must embrace the inevitable fact that change is an inherent part of life and not an option. It is a requirement, as is deepening our faith in the "process" by means of which change happens.

1. Explore your mind and heart and see if there is suffering in your life today. Don't confuse pain with suffering. Pain is a given in life; suffering is a choice that comes when we resist "what is," especially when it comes to change.
   - Consider that behind your physical or emotional pain could be a message that something needs to change in your life, and that you suffer when you resist accepting that change.
   - Remember, it is not impermanence that makes you suffer, it's wanting things to be permanent when

they are not. Seek to honor change—you'll suffer less.

2. Take a look at the opposite side of the dynamic of
   change by asking yourself, "Is there currently something in my experience that I am attached to seeing changed but, for whatever reason, it just isn't
   happening?

   • There is a popular saying among wine enthusiasts
     that goes, "We shall drink no wine before its time."
     There is wisdom in the idea that we can't force any-
     thing to fruition before its natural rhythm reveals
     its readiness.

   • The same wisdom applies to change. In your mind's
     eye, place the issue for which you desire change in
     a vintner's oak barrel. Visualize it as the energy
     of an idea "in process" and turn it over to the uni-
     verse. Let it go and "let God," trusting that when
     its time has come, the change shall come to pass.

3. Consider the "time machine" visualization. Travel
   back to a specific time in your past when a significant
   and challenging change was occurring.

- Observe the fact that while at the time you may have thought you were not going to survive, you made it through that transitional time.
- Get in touch with how that feels and key it into your current memory bank to draw from the next time change is at hand.

4. As a faith builder, place your hand over your heart and feel it beating.
   - Note that you do not doubt that the next beat will come. This is proof you already have faith in something larger than you that knows how to sustain you.
   - Now allow that faith to spill over into every area of your life trusting that the One who brought you here knows how to sustain you in and through whatever change is at hand . . . and breathe.

4.

THE WISDOM OF KNOWING
WHAT AND WHEN TO LET GO

Timing Is Everything

❧

Fruit drops from the tree when it is ready. Staying too long, or moving too early, misses the mark. The mark is the appropriateness that causes the fruit to fall when it is ready. . . . [T]he process has its own timing, and it creates changes in your life when those changes need to happen.

—GARY ZUKAV

We already know that change in life is a given. There is no way around this fact. The larger concern should be how we manage the process when it does happen. If we are conscious, we can perceive change in a manner that allows us to understand the deeper meaning, value, and purpose in the experience. When change is thrust upon us unexpectedly, we may be greatly challenged to see it as the appropriate doorway through which we must pass to our greater good. However, if we are to move forward in Earth School to "what can be," there comes a time when letting go of "what was" becomes a prerequisite. With mastering the art of uncertainty comes the necessary wisdom of knowing not only *what* to let go of, but also *when* to let it go. No doubt, this is a linear process in which timing plays a vital role. The good news is that contained within our karmic and spiritual DNA lies an inherent wisdom that knows far better than we when it is appropriate to release our grasp and let go of that to which we have been clinging. Our job is to bring ourselves into alignment with this inherent wisdom and trust the process.

I once talked to a man who was a professional trapeze artist and teacher. One day while teaching, he seriously injured his shoulder when the woman he was "catching" failed to let go of her trapeze at the right time. He had to hyperextend his arm to catch her, unexpectedly bearing all of her weight with his one arm. He said that if she had let go just *one second* sooner everything would have been fine. He went on to say that, being a fairly new student, she was probably afraid to let go. Had she been more focused on the rhythm between the two trapezes, it would have been a perfect release and catch. Rubbing his shoulder-slung arm he smiled and declared, "Timing is everything."

> All things entail rising and falling timing.
> You must be able to discern this.
>
> —MIYAMOTO MUSASHI

How true it is that when it comes to letting go of anything that has been deeply rooted in our lives, timing really is everything. We need only observe the rhythm of Life to know this is true. As we witness nature in "process" we will see that it is not a stagnant thing, but rather a vital life force always moving: a cyclic movement of things coming and going in a manner that requires letting go and honoring the process of change with grace and ease, making space for that which is to come. When undesired "shift" happens in our lives, it can be difficult to see the appropriateness in that change. If we were able to take a large enough step back and view the universe at work, we would be able to see the appropriateness in the natural rhythm of change moving through all that is; no one and no thing is exempt. Some things change appropriately slowly, so much so that we will never see the change in a visible way in our lifetime, such as mountain ranges rising and crumbling, or the giant redwood trees that grow for thousands of years before they return to the elements from which they came, only to spring up again as new seedlings. Nonetheless, they do change according to their own rhythm. Other changes, such as the coming

and going of the four seasons, are more obvious and, if
we are present enough in the moment to observe the appropriateness of those changes, we will see the perfection
of it all. Again, timing is everything. When we observe
Life closely, we can see that every living thing is hardwired with the innate wisdom to know when change
happens, not to resist it but to let go and flow with it.
The only difference between ourselves and nature is that
we need to be reminded that this is so. At the end of the
day, the wisdom of knowing when to let go is as important as knowing what to let go of. The good news is, this
wisdom lies within each of us and we are never too old
to access it on our journey into uncertainty.

MAKING SPACE FOR A
NEW LIFE TO BEGIN

> There are things that we never want to let go of,
> people we never want to leave behind. But keep in
> mind that letting go isn't the end of the world, it's
> the beginning of a new life.
>
> —AUTHOR UNKNOWN

Few things in life have more of an impact on us than the
inevitable changes that happen in our relationships. Stan

was an energetically spry gentleman in his early nineties. There was a twinkle in his clear periwinkle blue eyes, and he always dressed impeccably in a suit and tie and a sporty cap. One day he walked into my office and asked to talk to me. He was feeling very despondent. After sixty-five years of marriage he had been widowed for five years and was ready to "settle down" again. He declared he still had a lot of "good miles" left in him and didn't want to travel them alone. It turned out that he was quite the ladies' man and had no problems getting dates. His difficulty was that after one or two dates the women he courted didn't want to see him again, and he just couldn't understand why. He was truly heartbroken.

Stan invited me to come to his home for dinner so I could see how he lived, thinking perhaps his "honeys" didn't like his "pad." He was correct. As we ate dinner he talked a lot about his deceased wife. Then, while he proudly showed me through his home, it became apparent what his challenge was. In every room hung photographs of his beloved wife. Her clothes still hung in the closet. Earlier I had also noticed that Stan still wore his wedding band on his left hand, which was yet another sign that he had not made space in his mind, heart, or home for another relationship. It is safe to say the women he was courting got it immediately: He was not emotionally available. I shared my observations with him and, at his request, we talked a bit more. Then we did some affirmative prayer work around lovingly releasing his past relationship, as beautiful as it was, in order to create a new future. I know it was a huge moment of healing for Stan because I ran into him about six months later at the grocery store as he shopped arm-in-arm with his new fiancée.

> When I let go of what I am, I become what I might be.
> When I let go of what I have, I receive what I need.
>
> —TAO TE CHING

The wisdom of letting go has been taught throughout the ages. It has been said that there are no voids in life because the universe abhors a vacuum. While a quantum physicist could explain it in scientific terms, suffice it to say that the moment we let go of something, energy in one form or another must rush in to fill the void. The operative words here are "let go." As with Stan, too often we cling so tightly to what "has been" that we don't create that vacuum for what "can be." All the while, the universe is waiting patiently to fill the void we create by letting go. But we render it powerless to do so because we are still clinging to "what was." That is how powerful we are. While less perceptible than material things, thoughts and memories that tie us to the past can truly block our ability to create anything new, including relationships.

LETTING GO OF THE
NEED TO CONTROL

> If you want to reach a state of bliss . . . make a deci-
> sion to relinquish the need to control, the need to be
> approved, and the need to judge.
>
> —DEEPAK CHOPRA

Knowing who and what to let go of trying to control, and when to do so, is fundamental to our happiness. It seems to be an earth reality that most of us have "control issues" somewhere in our lives that need to be dealt with if we ever want to achieve authentic inner peace—the kind of peace that passes all understanding. Often we struggle to maintain control because to be out of control pushes us right to the edge of uncertainty and, as we know, most of us are not comfortable there. Often times we have an attachment to wanting to control people and their behavior when we really have little ability to do so. As an example, some of us may have an attachment to wanting to control our spouse or partner, our elderly parents or, at the other extreme, our adult children. As a result, we suffer. Some of us are attached to controlling other people's opinion of us, and in the process we sacrifice a piece of our authentic Self trying to live up to (or down to) their idea of who we are. As a result, we suffer. Some of us want to control how other people drive on the freeway. As a result, we suffer. Some of us would even like to control the stock market. As result, we suffer. The list could go on and on, couldn't it? Attachment to needing to control someone, some thing, or some event causes suffering. The illusion (and desire) to which most of us are attached is that we have control over much of what occurs in our lives. In actuality, we have control over very little beyond our next breath and thought. The good news is, our next thought *is* the point of entry wherein lies our inner peace.

THERE IS NO TIME LIKE NOW TO LAY YOUR STORY TO REST

Have you ever had an acquaintance tell you the same story about some trauma drama going in their life every time you were around them? Then one day the actual trauma drama ended, but the story lived on, taking on a life of its own, day after day, month after month, and yes, year after year, until it became a living legend. Eventually, that story turned into their history, becoming their point of identity, their trademark story that defines who they are in the world.

—From *The Art of Being: 101 Ways to Practice Purpose in Your Life*

There is no area in our lives, where change is involved, that letting go of something does not play a critical part, be it a relationship, a career, lifestyle, or (fill in the blank) _____. Sometimes it's not just holding on to wonderful memories of the past that keeps us from creating a new life today, it's clinging to old hurts, wounds, resentments, regrets, disappointments from the past, and, yes, expectations for the future. What I have noticed over my years as a teacher and spiritual mentor is how attached people can become to their stories that, most often, decry how someone or some situation or condition has caused them so much pain and suffering. Who can't relate to the allure of telling our stories. It's such a convenient way to avoid taking responsibility for our own lives and moving forward. What our stories generally have in common is the energy of either resentment, sadness, disappointment, regret, victimhood, judgment, or fear (or all the aforementioned) wrapped around them.

This is not to say that some of our stories are not sincerely legitimate and worthy of telling, once or maybe even twice.

Here is the problem: The stories we most often tell that keep us stuck are generally about something that happened in the past, also known as our history (hi-story). This is where the drama of "what was" is still very much alive in our minds, perhaps even long after the actual issue is dead and gone. The other place we get stuck is when we project ourselves into the future and breathe the breath of life into a story about something that may or may not, or should or should not, happen. In either case, letting go of those stories can be difficult because we draw so much power from telling them. It can be very seductive to tell our story to others who will listen because, lets face it, who doesn't love to "commiserate" (in this context, meaning to share their misery) with other like-minded people. It justifies our attachment to the drama. The interesting thing about telling our story over and over is that it becomes even more deeply ingrained in our minds each time we tell it, and the universe delights in keeping whatever we claim as our story alive. Soon enough that story takes on a life of its own and begins to define who we are. As we become comfortable with stepping into the unknown, where all new creation takes place, we will be more likely to want to leave our old stories behind. Just because they are part of our past doesn't mean they must become part of our future. The mystery of that which is yet to be does not have to be contaminated by that which has been. The awakening to this truth is when we can elect to tell a new kind of story. One that opens our minds and hearts to the infinite possibilities of a life worth living that lies ahead in the mystery of uncertainty.

LETTING GO OPENS THE PORTAL TO THE POWER OF PRESENCE

In Tibetan, "authentic presence" is *wangthang,* which literally means a "field of power" . . . The cause or the virtue that brings inner authentic presence is emptying out and letting go. You have to be without clinging.

—CHÖGYAM TRUNGPA

One of the benefits of letting go of our attachments to the past and the future, and the stories that keep us stuck there, is that it "empties us out." It allows us to be fully present and open in the moment, which is where our only true point of power lies patiently waiting for us. Several times a year I have the honor of conducting a daylong

"Mindfulness and Meditation" retreat at a beautiful 125-acre farm near where I live. Those who attend have an opportunity to empty themselves out. The ultimate purpose of this retreat is to offer tools and techniques to attendees that will assist them in aligning their minds and their bodies in the present moment, where the mystery and magic of Life is always waiting for them to open to its authentic presence. The power to begin a new life awaits each of us, as well, when we cease telling the stories that keep us stuck. There is a classic country song by Collin Raye with the title, "That's My Story (and I'm Stickin' to It)." For many people it could be titled, "That's My Story and It's Stickin' to Me." If you listen to yourself and others you may be surprised: We tend to tell the same old stories about our relationships, our jobs, our bodies, and other people, over and over. Perhaps it's time to get "unstuck" from our stories. Sometimes, we need some assistance in emptying ourselves out by letting our stories go.

> When we drop below our stories, we are led back
> to the mystery of here and now.
>
> —JACK KORNFIELD

As a way of assisting those who attended this retreat in being 100 percent emotionally available in the present moment, I create a mindfulness ritual that allows them to put their stories and endless mind-chatter to rest. At the beginning of the event I place a small box in front of the group and share a brief guided meditation on release. I then invite attendees to write on a piece of paper what-ever story or issue they may have brought with them that day that would keep them from being fully present at the retreat, in spirit, mind, and body. Then, as a ritual, I in-vite them to mindfully place the paper in the box, which I refer to as the "Great Box of Release."

At the end of a full day of mindfulness practices and meditations designed to open us to experiencing Life in the present moment, I tell the attendees that the box is really a miniature coffin. I request that they join me at a freshly plowed field in which I have previously dug a hole and, wherein, I've placed the box. I then perform a brief memorial service for all of the stories and affirmations of release placed in the box.

> We must be willing to let go of the life we have planned, so as to accept the life that is waiting for us.
>
> —JOSEPH CAMPBELL

During the memorial service I remind everyone that what they have each placed in the box is really the energy of their story and their intention to let it go, knowing that it was something that helped bring them to this moment in their life. Once we empty ourselves out and release pent-up energy, we automatically make space for some new form of energy to flow into our experience based on our current state of consciousness. As I conclude, I invite the attendees, if they wish, to take the shovel and help bury the box. There are always some tears and some joy in the process, but mostly there is a very strong sense of the sacred peace that reveals itself so effortlessly when we let go of what was or should be, trusting and knowing that the moment at hand bears a precious gift for us when we make space for it to be received.

Opening and closing, receiving and letting go, is the natural pulse beat of Life itself. It is the Universal Intelligence behind the heartthrob that animates, sustains, prospers, heals, grows, and evolves all things alive. As we awaken to this truth, aligning ourselves with the rhythm of its beat, knowing what to let go of and when to let it go comes naturally, with grace and ease. In short, living in the mystery and mastering the art of uncertainty becomes easy when we take our cue from this sacred continuum of Life . . . and we can learn to truly love it.

POINTS TO PONDER & PERSONALIZE

• As stated earlier in this chapter, when "shift" happens in your life it can be difficult to see the appropriateness in that change. At many points in your life, you will be faced with the need to embrace the wisdom of knowing not only *what* to let go of, but *when* to let go as well. As we discovered in the previous chapter, there is no area of your life where this is not true. Often the "what" is obvious because the change, while perhaps unexpected, has already transpired; such as in the case of the death of a loved one, or loss of a job due to economic conditions and downsizing, and so on. At other times, it may be a change you see coming, such as a pending retirement from a long-term career, a pending divorce, or a grown child moving into adulthood who, in the process, no longer appears to "need" you, and so on. In all of these cases, the "when" to let go is what needs to be understood. Sometimes, a grieving period is appropriate in bringing the "letting go" to a closure and release. This part of the process can require some time and should be honored if needed. These are the instances when seeking the support of a trained professional or your minister can be of great help. As you go through the process, you will be led to find the natural rhythm of Life that knows when it is appropriate to let go and move on. The operative words here are "move on."

• Can you relate at all to the story about my elderly friend, Stan? Relationships are only the starting point. The same question could apply to a job position that you may have held dearly at one time, but has long since passed. If you are ready for change to come about, but it just isn't happening, perhaps it's time to ask why. Maybe it's time to offer a final thanks for a relationship or job you had in the past that has left its imprint deeply etched upon your mind and heart (either positively or negatively), knowing that in this release process you are creating that vacuum that draws to you new relationships, or a job that reflects the love and passion you hold for life *today*.

• Have you ever caught yourself telling the same story over and over? If so, after reading this chapter, it's likely you may become even more aware of it when you are telling your story. Remember that each time you tell it (especially with feeling), it is becoming more deeply etched into the walls of your subconscious mind and your story begins to shape you, and how others see you as well. In short, your story begins to define who you are. Perhaps now would be the appropriate time to let go of your story. It's never too late to open your mind to a new story—one that is worthy of a life worth living.

• Do you have any "control issues" in your life? If so, can you see the pointlessness in them? Does your need to control people's behavior and the events and circumstances that go on around you cause you to suffer? If so, can you see the wisdom in releasing the need to control, now that you know you can't try to control and, at the same time, maintain inner peace? Are you willing to let go of the need to control now? If not now, when?

MINDFULNESS PRACTICES

Learning the skill of letting go is a lifetime practice. As you have discovered, there is no area of your life that is not affected negatively when you grasp and cling to the energy of life that occupies so many countless forms. The wisdom of knowing what you need to let go of, and when to let it go, lies patiently awaiting you as you open to it. That is the promise of the universe and it is waiting for a sign from you.

1. Take some time today and do a mental and physical inventory.
   - You may discover that you need to let go of old memories and old possessions that are essentially telling the universe there is no room to receive anyone or anything new.
   - Perhaps you know the "what" that needs to change, and now the "when" is just waiting for you to make the first move.
   - Remember, the universe abhors a vacuum, but you have to open and let go *before* you can receive.

2. The next time your need to control people, events, and circumstances pops up, ask yourself, "Am I more interested in trying to control the circumstances or having deep inner peace?"
   - Then take a deep breath . . . and let go. You'll be much happier, and so will those you have been trying to control.

3. Ann Landers wrote, "Hanging onto resentment is letting someone you despise live rent-free in your head." Today might be a good day to evict someone from your mind.
   - Are you willing to let them go? Perhaps, it's time to do some forgiveness work and be done with the toxic energy of resentment.
   - Remember, forgiving doesn't mean condoning past actions. It means setting yourself free to be an open and receptive vessel for joy today.

4. Do you feel a calling to drop down below your stories that no longer serve you in a healthy way, so that you might be led back to the mystery and magic of here and now, where the peace that passes all understanding patiently awaits your return?
   - Can you identify your favorite story to tell right now?
   - If so, all you need is a piece of paper, a small box, a shovel, and a bit of dirt.
   - Write your story on the paper, bless it, place it in the box, and give it a fit burial. You'll be amazed at the freedom it will bring you.

5

PLUMBING THE DEPTHS OF YOUR PURE POTENTIAL

The Deeper You Go, the More You'll Know

⚜

The Law of Pure Potentiality could also be called the Law of Unity, because underlying the infinite diversity of life is the unity of one all-pervasive spirit. There is no separation between you and this field of energy. The field of Pure Potentiality is your own Self. And the more you experience your true nature, the closer you are to the field of Pure Potentiality.

—DEEPAK CHOPRA

The closer we are drawn to living in the mystery of life and loving it, the closer we shall be to the potential and unlimited possibilities that come with awakening to our unity with Life. What we shall discover on the pathway of uncertainty is that creating a life worth living has no borders, boundaries, or barriers around it, other than the ones we erect ourselves. The ultimate realization is stepping into uncertainty with faith in our oneness with the Source and Its rewards; that is, the sky is the limit. In various wisdom teachings it is believed that every human being is born into a sea of Infinite Potential. Inherent within us lie the yet unrealized seeds of possibility for *anything* of which we can conceive. This is why it is of the utmost importance to think rightly: The seeds that grow and eventually sprout in our consciousness, which as we know must manifest in our lives, are the seeds that we nourish with our focus of attention and thought energy. The practice of a wise person is to mindfully water and fertilize the seeds of wholeness and a life worth living that comes from faithfully knowing we are one with the Source. With this idea in mind, I invite you to do this visualization:

Assume that you are dreaming and in your dream you see a giant lake—we will call it "Lake Potential." Think of the water in the lake as the unformed essence or energy of whatever you can imagine would make your life a life worth living. See yourself standing on the shore, staring at the lake, wishing you could jump into the limitless potential you know is there, but you don't know how to swim. So you walk away feeling "in want" and deprived of the infinite possibilities that lie within that unlimited potential. Then, suddenly you wake up from

your dream and you realize you are already fully immersed in the lake and always have been—you just
weren't aware of it.

Awakening to our true potential is our destiny as we
evolve spiritually. However, manifesting that potential
is a choice we will make, time and time again, based on
our understanding of our unity with the Source, and the
application of what Deepak Chopra refers to as the Law
of Pure Potentiality. Each of us was born in "Lake Potential," and it is as natural to us as is water to a fish. The
only difference is that a fish doesn't spend time searching
for water because it only knows water as a natural part
of its being; it has never been separated from the element
in which it was born and that very element effortlessly
sustains it with grace and ease. We, on the other hand,
seem to have no problem separating ourselves from the
natural element into which we were born, often spending a lifetime looking for our potential good somewhere
"out there" in the form of people, places, and things. Chopra refers to this external search as "object-referral"—
looking to the world as the source of our fulfillment,
which is always temporal at best. The alternative is what
he refers to as "Self-referral," which means we look to
Infinite Source for fulfillment, which can be found only
when we identify with the Self within that knows It is

unified with the Whole. In other words, when we turn
to the Self within, we naturally plunge into the Infinite
depths of Wholeness, where the mystery of that which is
yet to be assures us anything is possible.

> Our minds are finite, and yet even in these circum-
> stances of finitude we are surrounded by possibilities
> that are infinite, and the purpose of life is to grasp as
> much as we can out of that infinitude.
>
> —ALFRED NORTH WHITEHEAD

In its unformed state, our potential is the common
factor to be found in all possibilities; that is, until we
quantify them and put boundaries around them based on
our deepest beliefs. Some teachers refer to Infinite Potential as the cosmic glue that unifies the entire universe.
It can be a stunning discovery when we realize that we
are immersed in Its essence; we were born into it, as a
fish is born into water. Once we awaken to and access
our potential, we can bring it into form in specific ways
by means of conscious, creative, constructive, intentional,
and positive "possibility thinking and doing." These are
the thought seeds worth planting and nurturing in our
minds. The universe conspires for our infinitude of good
and the seeds for that good *already* lie within us in abundant supply, patiently waiting to be germinated. Perhaps,

that is what Kahlil Gibran had in mind when he wrote,
"A seed hidden in the heart of an apple is an orchard
invisible." Our true nature is realized when we understand that we are, literally, each "the apple" in the eye of
the Beloved, and that within us we hold untold potential. Now that we understand that we are swimming in
an ocean of Infinite Potential, the obvious question is:
"What type of seeds shall we be nurturing as we enter
through the gates of uncertainty and into the mystery of
that which is yet to be?"

> Spend every day listening to what your Muse is
> trying to tell you.
>
> —St. Bartholomew

I consider my Muse to be Spirit because she is ever
present, whispering in my ear; it's just that I am not always listening. When we listen to our Muse, we will be
given direct access to our Pure Potential, which is where
all new creation takes place. Before anything is manifest
and takes form in the relative (or material) world, it first
exists as the unformed energy of Pure Potential in the
unseen ethers of the Infinite. This includes everything we
can see, touch, taste, and hear. As an example, the chair
we might be sitting on was first an idea in someone's mind
before it became a chair. That chair was Pure Potential

before it took the form called chair; it only required someone to catch the idea in his or her mind and convert it into
wood, fabric, and so on.

The same could be said about any artistic creation as
well. As another example, before the song "Imagine" was
written and recorded by John Lennon, it was first the
unformed energy of Pure Potential just sort of floating
through the ethers until Lennon, in just the perfect moment, opened his consciousness, heard it, grabbed it, and
converted the energy of that idea as Pure Potential into
words and music. Lennon had made himself available
to the possibility of "Imagine" and because he was open
to hearing it, it flowed through his mind and heart. The
song itself was already a completed idea in the Infinite
Mind of the One. If his consciousness had not been open
to receiving "Imagine," it might very well have been
captured by me (don't I wish) or any other songwriter
who was aligned with the same energetic vibration that
drew the idea to him first.

The same can be said about any form of creation: We
are all energy converters who, by accessing our Pure
Potential, turn unformed possibilities into realities. The
hook is, we have to be totally and completely in the present moment and in touch with our Muse, or whatever
our idea is of that from whence comes our inspired
thoughts. We are already aware that nothing new can

ever be created from within the field of what we already know. Listening to our Muse means we must be willing to stand in the unknown because she does not linger in the past or the future, only the sacred moment of now, where anything is possible. Once again, welcome to the pathway of uncertainty—it's where our true Pure Potential awaits us.

THE POTENTIAL FOR GREATNESS IS NOT JUST FOR THE CHOSEN FEW

> Explore your mind, discover yourself, then give the best that is in you to your age and to your world. There are heroic possibilities waiting to be discovered in every person.
>
> —WILFRED A. PETERSON

When we look at people who have done or are doing great things in the world, it is obvious that they have, one way or another, accessed the seed potential of greatness from within and brought it to the surface. Whether we are talking about people, such as Bill Gates, Bono, Oprah, or the heroes of 9/11, sports megastars, entertainment icons, or just "everyday" people who have excelled in what they do, they accomplished that level of greatness by stepping into the unknown and unleashing the Infinite Potential with which they were born. Some people seem to discover their potential naturally at an early age and rise to greatness with apparent grace and ease, while others seem to manage to manifest greatness in their lives by virtue of their focused, disciplined, and intentional effort. Then there are those who are forced into greatness because they have no choice; conditions and events demand that they rise to the occasion at hand. We see that kind of greatness arise in the face of war, crisis, or emergencies (emerge-n-see the greatness) where something in the moment instantly and unexpectedly calls forward an extraordinary (*extra* ordinary) emergent power that we don't even know we have in us until that moment. Irrespective of how we arrive at it, the seed potential for greatness lies within everyone. It's not a matter of "getting" greatness, it's a matter of uncovering it, revealing it, and letting it out. Greatness is the potent energy of Life looking for an opening through which it may burst forth by means of each of us. Another way to think of it is that greatness is simply unformed Divine Potential seeking fullness of expression at Its own highest level. In the words of Ernest Holmes, "Your soul belongs to the universe. Your mind is an outlet through which the Creative Intelligence of the universe seeks fulfillment." *You* are the instrument for greatness.

> Greatness is a road leading towards the unknown.
>
> —CHARLES DE GAULLE

Living in greatness will always bring us to the edge of uncertainty. Our biggest challenge with our inherent potential for greatness might be that too often we unconsciously fear it because we have not "conditioned" ourselves for what greatness may bring. That subtle fear will cause us to avoid our potential for greatness by keeping us stuck in the trenches of "the norm," which is to say, our mundane daily existence, keeping our heads well below the line of fire where we believe it's safe. It's true, greatness will require that we rise above the norm, one way or another, whether we are pulled by inspiration or pushed by pain. It's about our being willing to be that outlet through which Life seeks to give birth to the greatness It is. In the process of accessing our true potential, we naturally create something new and powerful. This, in turn, may lead us to the edge of uncertainty where we are given yet another opportunity to soar into the possibilities only to be discovered in the mystery of the unknown. So, the question is: Where in our life is greatness waiting to burst forth? For many of us it could be as close as our very next breath, but we often fail to see it. Are we really willing to be at that place where our greatest potential manifests in the human condition? Are we willing to step up and out of the trenches and *be* greatness in action? How can we tell when our greatness is ready to emerge? We'll know because the emergent energy of greatness will dissolve all sense of separation from Life in a single heartbeat.

> Seek not greatness, but seek truth and you will find both.
>
> —HORACE MANN

Over the years, we all develop reasonably good skills in one area or another that offer us the opportunity to tap into our Divine Potential, becoming the willing vessel through which Life may find fuller expression. Admittedly, while some things have come much easier for me than others, there are those magical times when, irrespective of what I am doing, I am so deeply involved in it that I seem to slip into a state of grace and ease; the doing becomes quite effortless, as if the thing I am doing is actually "doing me." I know we all have had such moments. I believe those are the moments when our inher-

ent greatness reveals itself; it's when our Divine Potential
is realized in the human condition. From a spiritual perspective, those are the moments when we actualize our
oneness with the universe, and our "doingness" seamlessly merges with our "beingness." Abraham Maslow
might refer to this as a peak experience—those moments
when we become fully one with the activity in which
we are engaged and all sense of apartness or separation
from the Whole dissolves. For me, I wish I could say that
those moments were more frequent than they are. However, what I have learned is that as I continue to evolve
spiritually, becoming more sensitized to the alignment
of my spirit, mind, and body, I can generally tell when
one of those moments of "greatness" is about to emerge—
I can feel it coming. It happens in those moments when
I feel most fully alive, doing what I know I am meant to
be doing in that holy instant, which can and does change
day to day. Perhaps Horace Mann is correct: When we
seek the truth of our oneness with the Whole, our greatness cannot help but come as part of the experience. The
closer we live to the center of the hub of our Being, the
more our inherent potential is actualized and expressed
uniquely as you and me. Practicing the art of uncertainty
brings us nearer to the center of the hub where our Pure
Potential awaits us—it's a practice worth pursuing, yes?

PEELING OFF THE LABELS

(*Your Redefining Moment*)

Others can give you a name or a number, but they can never tell you who you really are. That is something you yourself can discover from within.

—Thomas Merton

Few things are more damaging, repressing, and restrictive to the unique expression of our Divine Potential than the labels that have been placed upon us by others, or we have placed upon ourselves. From the day we are born we begin accumulating labels, many of which we had no say in. The problem with labels is that they instantly invite the world to define (judge) us, starting with labels such as our gender, and even our name. With labels come expectations, and with expectations come confinement and too often, shame. Søren Kierkegaard wrote, "Once you label me you negate me." While we are still young children and open, we are given many unsolicited opinions of who we are (or should be) by family, friends, strangers, teachers, and ministers, as well as the media. Because we don't know better, we allow these opinions to further label us as tall, short, fat, skinny, beautiful, homely, smart, stupid, talented, not talented, rich, poor, white, brown, black, yellow, gay, straight, and so on. Another popular label is, boys are "supposed" to act one way and girls another. This label alone has repressed the potential of countless human beings for millennia. As we mature, even our age (too old or too young) becomes yet another label we are forced to wear. Such is the process of becoming a human being in our culture. Depending on one's perspective, none of this is either good or bad. It simply means that from the day we are born, who we believe ourselves to be is actually defined by others. As those labels accumulate, the unique beings we were sent to planet earth to be become encased, layer upon layer, in other people's truth shrouding our true potential. Stepping into the mystery of that which is yet to be can be our redefining moment because it's when and where anything is potentially possible—we simply need to be willing to peel away the labels and acknowledge who we uniquely are.

TO DISCOVER WHO WE ARE
WE MUST FIRST DISCERN
WHO WE ARE NOT

What each must seek in his life never was on land or
sea. It is something out of his own unique potentiality for experience, something that never has been and
never could have been experienced by anyone else.

—JOSEPH CAMPBELL

Regardless of how old we may be chronologically, it's
never too late to redefine who we believe ourselves to
be. It may require we walk through an emotional mine-
field of uncertainty to get there but the effort is well
worth the undertaking. To discover who we are we must
first discern who we are not. As we mature spiritually,
we can choose to peel away the labels that don't honor
who we discover our real selves to be. One of the most
empowering moments comes when we realize that while
we did not have absolute control over what went into our
minds as children, as adults we do. At any given moment,
we can choose to reject the labels that others may have
slapped on us throughout our lifetime, as well as the ones
we erroneously placed on ourselves. I recall reading many

Dr. Seuss books to my daughter when she was a toddler, *before* she had too many labels placed upon her by the world and, yes, by me as well. One of the passages I still remember to this day goes, "Today you are You, that is truer than true. There is no one alive who is Youer than You." Along with some additional help from Mr. Rogers, *Sesame Street*, and a spiritual grounding from the day she was born, I think she got it: Twenty-six years later, every time I look at her, I see a happy, self-reliant, self-expressed, authentic human being, and my heart swells because I know *she* knows who she is.

When we discover who we are and live from that true identity, the only opinion that will matter is our own. As we awaken to this awareness, we have the opportunity to redefine ourselves from the inside out. What is your *real* identity? Underneath all the labels, who are you *really*? In truth, who you are, and who you have always been, is an individualized expression of God. Is this yet another opinion and label? Sure it is, so keep peeling away. Underneath all the labels lies the indescribable Divine Potential that will open every door of Self-discovery you happen upon while on your journey to the place you really never left, which is your oneness with the universe.

ARE YOU SINGING YOUR SONG?

Everyone has talent. What is rare is the courage to
follow the talent to the dark place where it leads.

—ERICA JONG

In my early lean days as a musician while attending college, one of the things I did to earn money was to teach
music. My students ranged from eight to eighty years of
age and, while it varied greatly, quite often the degree
of their natural talent was very high. What I found most
frustrating was that, in many cases, I was able to recognize their potential even though they could not see it in
themselves. After a few months of lessons some students
would throw in the towel, offering excuses such as, "I'm
too old (or too young) to learn how to sing or play the
piano or guitar," or "these drums just take up too much
space in my home." I believe that for at least some of
them, beyond any resistance to the commitment to practice daily, their own fear held them back. We held recit-
als every six months and that would nudge them out of
the box of their comfort zone. I saw so much awesome
talent and potential choked back by fear and uncertainty.
Had I known then what I know now about the Law of
Pure Potentiality and the infinite field of possibilities to

be found by consciously embracing uncertainty, I would have worked harder at getting some of my students to come to the edge and lean over.

> Most men lead lives of quiet desperation and go to
> the grave with the song still in them.
>
> —HENRY DAVID THOREAU

The song Thoreau is speaking of is the unexpressed Self, the creative essence of Spirit seeking an outlet. What I learned from my students, and from the pursuit of my own career as a writer and performer, was that it requires courage to "sing our song." That courage will, indeed, take us to the very edge of uncertainty—our comfort zone—that dark place Erica Jong speaks of where fear lingers; that is, fear of rejection, fear of failure, and perhaps even fear of success. The only thing worse than failing at something is succeeding and not feeling worthy of the success. Remembering the universal principle of success and the Yes factor, we can faithfully choose to consciously lean into the fear, knowing that we are guided every step of the way because Spirit is right there with us. Following the creative nudge into the dark places of the unknown is where our potential to soar confidently into the mystery of that which is to be awaits us.

ATTACHMENT TO APPROVAL
STIFLES OUR POTENTIAL

> Be who you are and say what you feel, because those
> who mind don't matter and those who matter
> don't mind.

> —Dr. Seuss

Fear of rejection by others seems to be an issue most all
of us will have the opportunity to heal if we are going to
access our potential and be fully expressed in bringing the
gift of who we are to life. It's like "Oh, what will I do if
they don't like my song?" Get over it! You are singing
your song for *you*, not them. Some of us have held back
singing our own song because we were too busy trying
to sing the song someone else thought we should be singing. When we try to sing someone else's song, it sounds
like "tinkling brass," that is, it will not be authentic, and
our soul knows it. That is when our sense of purpose for
being alive begins to wither and die. Perhaps that is what
Emerson meant when he wrote, "There comes a time in
every man's education when he arrives at the conviction
that envy is ignorance, that imitation is suicide."

If we truly listen to our hearts we'll hear our song

calling. It will be different for each of us, and it should be because the Universe doesn't need two of anything exactly the same. Our "song" may not be music at all, but it will draw upon our Divine Potential and give greater expression to our soul. Perhaps most importantly, it will be something that enriches not only our lives, but the lives of others and the world. Our song will serve as a portal through which Pure Potential and the uniqueness of *our* soul flows onto the stage of life. How will we know when we are singing our own song? We'll each become a vessel for unbridled joy, and time will appear to stand still . . . and we shall look down only to notice that, in that sacred moment of bliss we have leapt off the edge, and we are soaring.

POINTS TO PONDER & PERSONALIZE

- I encourage you to reread the visualization regarding "Lake Potential" and consider the following: Do you see yourself standing and looking longingly at the possibilities of a life worth living "out there" or do you see yourself already as one with Infinite Potential? Can you relate to the idea that inherent within you are the seeds of possibility for *anything* of which you can conceive? "Infinite Potential" means that *all* possibilities exist, waiting for you to give form to them. Understanding that the seeds that will grow and eventually sprout in your consciousness are the ones that you nourish with your focus of attention and thought energy, what seeds are you nurturing on a daily basis? Are they life-affirming seeds that will expand your sense of wholeness? If not, it's not too late to nurture the seeds that will.

- Can you see the potential for greatness within you? Remember, you were born with that potential; it's a matter of revealing it. Can you pinpoint any moments throughout your life when that greatness within was demonstrated? Have you ever had a "peak moment" experience . . . perhaps while participating in sports or the performing arts? You may have had a moment of greatness in an emergency or crisis. If you can remember even one time when your greatness emerged, you may be assured it is still there.

- Are you willing to claim this as your redefining moment? Have there been labels placed on you that have caused you to feel separate and apart from your true potential? Can you see how those labels have kept you from being all you might be? Are you willing to challenge the "authority" of whoever placed those labels on you by beginning to remove them, even if *you* were the one who put them there? The mere idea of pulling off your labels may strike fear in your heart because of one of two things: First, you may fear gaining the disapproval of those who originally placed the labels there and, second, you may fear that without those labels you won't know who you are. As you pull the labels away take a deep breath and realize it is your moment of liberation from the opinions of others. Who you will discover underneath all of the labels is who you *really* are: A sacred being (what's not to like about that?) with direct access to the Pure Potential that comes with unifying with the One. You don't have to earn your potential because it's yours by divine appointment. As the great teacher said, "It is the Father's good pleasure to give you the Kingdom." The question now is: "What shall you do with all that Divine Potential?" The mystery awaits you to come to the edge.

- Are you able to discern your song—the gift that you have brought to share with your earth family? If so, are you sharing it? If you have not yet discovered it, perhaps your "unsung song" is painting, writing, dancing, learning another language, becoming an entrepreneur, public speaking, teaching, photography, sewing, juggling, a new job skill, volunteering, gardening, gourmet cooking, or (fill in the blank) _____. The possibilities are literally infinite. Regardless of what "your song" might be, make a commitment to open yourself to the Divine Potential inherent in you. You will not fully discover your gifts until you are first willing to fearlessly share them with the world. The world is waiting for you and the gift you bring.

MINDFULNESS PRACTICES

Ray Charles wrote, "There are many spokes on the wheel of life. First, we're here to explore new possibilities." To explore anything means going where we have never been before. When it comes to new possibilities for our lives, whether the exploration is an inner journey or an outer one, it is a call to step into the unknown. These Mindfulness Practices will help you to plumb the depths of your own "Lake Potential."

1. One of the greatest challenges we often have in accessing our Pure Potentiality is that it requires a quiet mind to plumb its depths. As a Mindfulness Practice, I invite you to take time to contemplate your unity with Life.

- Dedicate time for meditation each day and spend some time in nature to observe the Law of Pure Potentiality being demonstrated perfectly: Animals, trees, and flowers are incapable of separating themselves from their Source and, as a result, in their natural element they thrive. Become the silent witness—watch and learn, and in so doing come more into alignment with your own true nature.

- Clear your mind and heart of all negative thinking that would cause you to feel separated from others or from the Source. Focus on healing all sense of apartness from Life. Know you were born in Lake Potential, as a fish is to water. Focus on your breath and see yourself floating effortlessly in the Essence of Life. How does it feel to be immersed in Pure Potential? Key in to that feeling and remember it the next time you are feeling separate and apart from the Source within. You don't have to go outside of yourself to find your potential, you have to dive into your Self.

2. Begin to explore the many labels that have been placed on you by others, or that you have placed on yourself. To explore means to go where you have

never gone before—to willingly step into the mystery of uncertainty and see what you find.

- Explore any areas of your life where you may be drawing your sense of identity from those labels. Contemplate who you might be without any labels. Are you willing to take a peek and see?
- This could be your redefining moment, and this is what the art of uncertainty is all about. The possibilities you will find will set you free to soar.

3. What shall you choose to do with the gift of your Pure Potential today? The possibilities are endless. Is it your time to come to the edge of that dark place of uncertainty and transcend any fear of sharing your gift with the world?

- Begin by making a commitment to share the passion, talent, or creative self-expression you have been holding back from the world with at least three people. This will prime the pump and get the juices flowing.
- Not to worry, Infinite Presence, the ultimate Source of Light, is right there with you; so go ahead . . . you've got the spotlight. Sing your song for all you're worth!

6.

FAILURE IS NOT AN OPTION

The Yes Factor Never Sleeps

❧

I have not failed 1,000 times. I have successfully dis-
còvered 1,000 ways to not make a lightbulb.

—THOMAS EDISON

Here is a question for you, and I invite you to ponder it for a moment before you read any further
than this paragraph: What would you attempt to do in
the future if you knew you could not fail? More specifically, would you be willing to walk forward on the path
of uncertainty to discover new possibilities for your life
if you knew that, regardless of what you tried, you would
find success awaiting your arrival?

Be careful how you interpret the world: It is like that.

—ERICH HELLER

The topic of success and failure came up recently in
a conversation I was having with one of my mentoring

clients. He was about ready to throw in the towel on a new business venture that had taken him way out of his comfort zone. He commented that it didn't much matter which business strategies he tried in getting this new venture off the ground; he failed. He said, in fact, failure had been a lifelong challenge for him in just about everything he did, and he concluded with the statement, "Sometimes life just doesn't seem fair." That is when I hooked his attention by telling him that life is never fair or unfair, but rather, it is how we choose to see life that determines our experience of it. I said to him, "You have not really been failing at all. In actuality, you have been succeeding splendidly at what the world has labeled 'failing.'" Perspective is everything, isn't it?

Arnold Schwarzenegger is credited with having said, "Failure is not an option; everyone has to succeed." According to the universal Law of Cause and Effect (from this point forward to be referred to as simply "the Law"), he is absolutely correct. The universe operates solely on the principle of success, which I refer to as the "Yes" factor: It takes your deepest thoughts and beliefs about yourself and life and, if it could speak, it would say, "Yes, if this is what you believe, I can only agree with you, so now let me help you succeed in proving you are correct." It doesn't matter if the beliefs you hold are life-affirming and positive, or self-defeating and negative. Either way the universe conspires to help you succeed in bringing those beliefs to fruition. This is not new information: In 470 BC, Buddha said, "All that we are is the result of what we have thought. The mind is everything. What we think we become." Hundreds of years later another great teacher came along and said the same thing, but differently: "It is done unto you as you believe." In both cases, this is the "Yes" factor in action.

> It's not what you know about the Law that matters . . . it's what you do with what you know about the Law that matters.
>
> —DMJ

While most aficionados of affirmative thinking already understand this is how the universe works, I wonder how many of us actually stop and take time to look at those areas in our lives that appear not to be working as well as we might like, and then realize we really are succeeding at failing. This is not meant to be a pithy statement; it is how the Law works. In *The Science of Mind,* Ernest Holmes described how absolutely singular this one Law is in Its purpose, and how It can create such diverse results, when he wrote: "It is around us in Its original state, ready and willing to take form through the impulse of our creative belief. It works for us by flowing through us . . . we can use it correctly only as we understand It and use It according to Its nature. Hence, it follows that if we believe that It will not work, It really does work by appearing to 'not work.' When we believe it will not, then, according to the principle, It *does not*. But when It does not, It still does—only It does according to our belief that It will not." While this is a bit of a tongue twister from Holmes, just for a moment, stop and think about the implications of his statement: It is an unconditional guarantee from the universe that failure is not an option. In essence, there is only one Creative Law and we use that Law in many different ways every day of our lives.

> For to everyone who has, more shall be given, and he will have an abundance; but from the one who does not have, even what he does have shall be taken away.
>
> —MATTHEW 25:29

At times, life truly can seem unfair. When we live unconsciously, we are unaware of the Yes factor, thus it can be easy to feel victimized by life and outer circumstances. We look around and see that while some people seem to be doing fine, others appear, according to our own perspective and judgment, not to be doing so fine. It seems as if life has singled some people out to succeed at succeeding, while others are singled out and doomed to succeed at failing, and that is not the case. To say that life is either fair or unfair, and that it treats some more favorably than others, is to declare that the Law, which is a universal principle, is whimsical and judgmental, and it is not. It operates consistently the same for everyone, just as the sun shines, or the rain falls, equally on each of us. The important thing to remember is that as we step into the mystery of that which is to be, the Yes factor is right there with us.

> Ignorance of the law, which everybody is supposed to know, does not constitute an excuse.
>
> —LEGAL MAXIM

There is an interesting parallel between the universal Law and our civil law. In both instances, ignorance of them is no excuse for violating them and, in both instances, we are held accountable when we do violate them. I recall once, while attending college, getting caught in a traffic speed trap where a police officer with a radar gun clocked me going 55 miles per hour in a 45-mile-per-hour zone. I never saw him, nor, for that matter, did I see any nearby signs declaring it a 45-mile-per-hour zone. When I pulled over, I asked him why he chose to stop me when there were at least three other cars around me going the same speed. He grinned, shrugged his shoulders, and replied, "I don't play favorites—why not you?" Not wanting to feel victimized and having just completed a marketing class called The Skill of Effective Negotiating, I thought I would try to talk him out of giving me the ticket. While looking him directly in the eyes, in my most authoritative voice, I told him it didn't seem fair, that I was only keeping up with the flow of traffic, and that I had absolutely no idea that I was in a 45-mile-per-hour zone because I saw no visible signs posted. He politely smiled a toothy grin and nodded his head while replying, "I am sure you didn't, and here's your ticket. You have a nice day now." Clearly, the "It's not fair" clause had no effect on him. Likewise, our ignorance of the universal Law and how it functions has no more affect on the Yes factor than does our ignorance of the speed limit in getting us out of a traffic ticket. In both cases, our ignorance has automatic consequences. As we take responsibility for ourselves by realizing that we are always becoming "cause" to our own "effect," we shall understand that we are not punished *for* our mistakes, but *by* them.

> The Law can be either our servant or our master, depending on how consciously we approach it and how wisely we make use of its awesome power.
>
> —FROM *How to Speak Science of Mind*

If we are conscious, attentive, curious, and inquisitive we will see that we are continually being given opportunities to examine the different areas in our lives where we can witness the Law working flawlessly according to our deepest beliefs. As an example: We may be succeeding in a rewarding manner in our relationships because we have a positive prototype in our belief system of what a healthy relationship looks like. However, when it comes to prosperity we may be succeeding at failing because we have an unhealthy prototype in our belief system based on a sense of shame and lack of self-worth. It is important for us to see and understand that this is the same Law, manifesting as two different results. In both cases, the Yes factor is simply doing its job. While the results may appear to vary, it's not because the universe is inconsistent in its adherence to the Law, it's because we are. Failure is not an option. The Law is the principle of success in motion and, as Buddha inferred, our mind directs where it goes. This means that we can use the Law in a manner that changes how success shows up in our life. Simply put, when we become mindfully aware of the Law and how it operates, we also become its master. Henry Ford was correct when he said, "Whether you think you can or whether you think you can't, you're right." As you contemplate the mystery of uncertainty regarding some specific aspect of your future, what do you think you can do . . . or can't do?

PUTTING THE YES FACTOR TO WORK, *CONSCIOUSLY*

> Argue for your limitations and sure enough, they're yours.
>
> —RICHARD BACH

Understanding how the Yes factor functions in our daily life is really quite simple: The universe agrees with whatever we hold in consciousness as our deepest beliefs, and it conspires to make them our reality. On the other hand, it's quite another thing to be diligent enough in our daily lives to be conscious of the number of ways we put the Yes factor to work without even being aware we are doing so.

As an example, few will disagree with the fact that we are being pummeled daily by the media with how "bad" things are. If we are not mindful, it's easy to be seduced into agreeing with that opinion because the evidence seems to be so overwhelming. It's right there in front of us and so many people are agreeing with it, it "must" be true. Unfortunately, in the process, the Yes factor is at

work, affirming it is done unto each of us as we believe—
and the cycle goes unbroken. If we pay close attention to
the words that come out of our mouths, we might amaze
ourselves at how often we catch ourselves agreeing with
the prognosticators of doom. If we can become witness
to our own thoughts and words, we may hear them reflected in our conversations with others. One of the reasons it is so inviting to agree with negative news, especially
in the company of others, is that it makes the things we
may be dealing with that are less than wonderful more
acceptable. In other words, it helps us feel better about
feeling bad.

The problem with identifying too closely with what's
wrong with our lives and the world is that, when we buy
into that belief, it is like baiting the trap of a self-fulfilling
prophesy into which we then step: The Yes factor has no
alternative but to hold us hostage in the dungeon of our
own mind and beliefs. Truly, when we argue for our
limitations they begin to take on a life of their own that
guarantees us great success at staying stuck in the muck
and the mire of the six-o'clock news. It doesn't have to
be that way. Rather than arguing for our limitations by
buying into what the purveyors of doom may be selling,
we can celebrate our possibilities by remembering we are
one with a universe that always affirms for us that which
we affirm for ourselves. The more fully we realize our

oneness with Life, the more clear it will become that we are not failures, nor have we ever been—it is a universal impossibility. This is powerful and crucial information to embody as we delve more fully into the art of uncertainty. In short, what do you think you can or cannot do with your life in the future? Think again, and know that either way, you are right.

POINTS TO PONDER & PERSONALIZE

• The term "perspective is everything" has been around for a long time, and it has been used as a wisdom mantra by people who know enough about the way the universe works to understand there is always another way to perceive what is taking place. When it comes to the Yes factor, if it appears that you are failing at some endeavor, can you see the wisdom in looking at that situation with new eyes? Don't view your circumstance as a failure. On the contrary, congratulate yourself and, as odd as it may seem, celebrate your failure. It is a very empowering way to lay claim to your awesome ability to create. Get excited because, as negative as it may appear, you have demonstrated the success principle perfectly. Now it's time to use the Yes factor *consciously*, knowing a different result is already on the way.

- It starts with changing how you see yourself in the world. Anaïs Nin wrote, "We don't see things as they are, we see them as we are." What image of yourself are you currently projecting onto the screen of life? Understand that when you start referring to yourself as a success, the universe doesn't ask in what way are you a success, it is merely waiting for you to make that decision and place it in the projector of your mind. What ideas about a life worth living would you bring to the edge of uncertainty if you knew you could not fail?

- Can you relate at all with my experience in receiving the traffic ticket? Does understanding that "ignorance is no excuse" when it comes to violating the Yes factor help you in moving out of the victim role? To that end, if your perspective has been that "life isn't fair," I lovingly quote my dear ol' mom's response to me as a kid whenever I droned that sentiment: "Honey, the Fair is in Pomona . . . get over it and get on with it." Life may not always seem fair but it is continuously offering us the opportunity to prove it is wonderful and to get on with making it so.

- Remember, you are hardwired to succeed. The universe is listening, and it has already said "Yes." This marks the beginning of a whole new experience on your journey into the mystery of the unknown because now you understand that failure is not an option. How will you choose to see yourself in the future? William Shakespeare wrote, "There is nothing either good or bad but thinking makes it so." Perspective really *is* everything.

MINDFULNESS PRACTICES

Understanding that the Yes factor is the universal Law of Cause and Effect in motion puts you in the position of being a conscious co-creator with the universe. Understanding that energy moves in whichever direction your thoughts travel frees you to introduce new intentions that will transform any limiting ideas of failure into success. Do these mindfulness practices with the awareness that in every moment the Yes factor is your personal servant awaiting your command.

1. Take a piece of paper and draw a vertical line down the middle. On the left side make a list of the areas in your life that, up until now, you may have labeled as "failure." It could be in the area of business, finances,

relationships, health, fitness, and so on. Then, on the right side of the paper do the same process; however, this time address the areas in your life that you might label as a "success." Then go down both sides of the list, and with each item ask yourself these questions:

a) Can I see the impartiality of the Yes factor working on both sides of this list?

b) Understanding that the Yes factor is working equally on both sides of the list, have I unconsciously been taking the "successes" in my life for granted and focusing more on the failures? (Remember, the Law goes where you focus your attention.)

c) Have I unknowingly been arguing for my limitations by justifying why things are the way they are rather than challenging them?

d) Have I been settling for certain limitations, and the restrictions they bring, rather than challenging them and moving in a proactive manner to improve them?

e) Are there any underlying beliefs on this list that affirm that life isn't fair, or that I see myself as a victim of circumstances? (Remember, victims are powerless over their situation—it's time to reclaim your power.)

2. The course of action you can take lies inherent in the questions themselves. The practice is to make a choice every moment of the day to live more fully conscious of the role the Yes factor is playing 24/7.

   • Be certain you are not directing your attention to what, until now, you (or the world) may have labeled as a failure.

   • Be willing to conduct conscious self-inquiry on an ongoing basis and challenge your beliefs.

   • By being conscious and present in the moment, you can catch yourself as you start to argue for your limitations. When you do, repeat the following affirmation with feeling and conviction: "I am the Law of success in motion, and I now choose to succeed in a new way. I now name it, I claim it, and I believe it."

Remember, failure is not an option—the Yes factor guarantees it is so.

7.

HANDLE YOUR HABIT
ENERGY CONSCIOUSLY

Rising from the Rut

As long as habit and routine dictate the pattern of
living, new dimensions of the soul will not emerge.

—HENRY VAN DYKE

In his enlightening book *The Heart of the Buddha's Teaching*, Vietnamese Buddhist monk Thich Nhat Hanh
writes, "There is a story in Zen circles about a man and
a horse. The horse is galloping quickly, and it appears
that the man on the horse is going somewhere important. Another man, standing alongside the road, shouts,
'Where are you going?' and the first man replies, 'I
don't know! Ask the horse!' This is also our story. We
are riding a horse, we don't know where we are going,
and we can't stop. The horse is our habit energy pulling
us along."

In the introduction of this book, I suggested that a rut is like a grave with no ends. While there is a certain amount of comfort to be found by staying in the rut, where redundancy is the way of life, if we do we will never enter the mystery of the unknown, where new creation, purpose, and meaning awaits us. Our soul nature patiently awaits us to ascend from the "grave" of the rut so that we can get on with unfolding who we have come here to be—spiritually, emotionally, and physically. Because of their repetitive nature, many of our most firmly ingrained habits will not only keep us in that rut, they will dig it deeper. Simply put, the deeper the rut, the more our unbridled habit energy will have its way with us, pulling us along wherever it may choose to go. It doesn't have to be that way.

Do you have any habits? Of course that is a rhetorical question because we all have habits. If I were to ask you to write down the habits that most quickly come to mind, more than likely you would list your bad habits first. The probability is that you also have more than a few good habits; it's just that the bad ones seem to more obviously "run amok," pulling us in every which way, which is why they tend to come to mind first. My dictionary defines a habit as "An acquired behavior pattern regularly followed until it has become almost involuntary." Nowhere in that definition does it say that a habit, in and of itself, is good or bad. Clearly, the proof is in the proverbial pudding: What makes a habit either good or bad for us, personally, is the result of said behavior and how it serves us in creating a life that we feel worthy of . . . or not. Even if we are not always consciously aware of our habits, they are there operating as if they had a life of their own, independent from our thinking mind.

Staying with the horse metaphor, perhaps the real question is not so much, "Do you have habits," but rather, "Are you riding them in a direction that is taking you closer to, or further from, the life *you* dream of having?" This is where being fully conscious on your journey into uncertainty becomes crucial because your future depends on your ability to choose wisely the horse you wish to ride. Changing the direction in which the horse is moving is simple if you know how and, while it's not always easy, it *is* well worth the effort. As you will see, transforming bad habit energy into good habit energy can serve you well on the journey into the mystery of that which is yet to be.

> Our self-image and our habits tend to go together. Change one and you will automatically change the other.
>
> —Dr. Maxwell Maltz

Any pattern of behavior you *regularly* follow will eventually result as a habit because it is energy moving in a specific direction at your command *until* it becomes deeply etched into the walls of your consciousness, where it seemingly then takes on a life of its own. This is true of good habits, such as brushing your teeth every day or kissing a loved one hello or good-bye, as well as bad habits, such as gossiping or mindlessly eating unhealthy food. Because a large majority of your consciousness is "warehoused" in the subconscious mind, there is plenty of space for habit energy to operate without your awareness that it is doing so. The habits operating in your life, conscious or unconscious, good or bad, are serving you in projecting your current self-image onto the screen of your life. In other words, working deductively from effect back to cause, if you look at your habits you can track them back to how you really feel about yourself. This is true of both your good and bad habits.

As a place to begin, you need look no further than your own home to witness how habit energy, unexamined and unchallenged, keeps you from evolving into the person you came here to be. It will show up in the type of food you eat and the manner in which you eat it, as well as other substances you may put into your body, such as alcohol and drugs. Your habit energy will reveal itself in how you maintain the health of your physical body and, perhaps even more so, the body of your relationships.

> In short, the habits we form from childhood make no small difference, but rather they make all the difference.
>
> —ARISTOTLE

Often times we avoid confronting our lifelong habits because they are comfortable and it's easier to stay with them than manage the discomfort confronting them will bring. The minute we decide to deal with a negative habit head-on it will automatically force us onto the edge of uncertainty, where we will have to deal with the unknown change it may bring.

A close friend I've known since we were both youngsters called me about a year ago to announce that he and his live-in partner of several years were going to call it quits and go their separate ways (again). "We just cause each other pain and sorrow. We are not good for each other and I have no love for her in my heart whatsoever," he declared. I remained silent and listened to his story regarding the latest dispute that triggered his decision (this time). After about ten minutes, I reminded him that this was precisely the same story I had heard many times, not only for the past few years, but for the past forty years regarding every woman he had ever had a relationship with. So, I was already intimately familiar with all the details: Over the past four decades he had gone through numerous relationships, continually drawing to him essentially the same person each time, only with a different name and hair color. After I'd made my case, he chuckled, stopped talking, and took a deep breath. I knew that he understood immediately that I was not trying to be intentionally cruel or unsupportive, but that I was simply calling him on his ongoing habit of addiction to toxic relationships. In the past several years, he and his partner had created a relationship that, as unfulfilling and painful as it had become, was easier to stay in than it was to break the habit they had become to each other. As an epilogue to the drama, they did end up going their separate ways and within six months my friend again had another live-in partner . . . and the cycle goes unbroken, as does the horse of his habit energy.

My friend's ongoing relationship dramas exemplify how we all are subject to developing habits in our lives that can become toxic (and similarly addictive) if we are not mindful of the subtleties that come with living in the relative comfort of the rut rather than doing the necessary work to move beyond its confines. In a curious sort of way, staying stuck in a habit is the ultimate form of immediate gratification because it creates a diversion that redirects the flow of the creative life force away from our true feelings, where we would be forced to deal with them. Then, almost effortlessly, the habit energy sublimates into mindless activities that often result in unproductive lifestyles, unhealthy bodies, and relationships filled with sadness, pain, and suffering. If we want to effect a change in the direction our habit energy flows, coming to the edge of uncertainty is not an option.

> To fall into a habit is to begin to cease to be.
> —MIGUEL DE UNAMUNO

A part of us dies when any negative habit becomes a mindless activity, especially when we continue to do it because it's easier (or less painful) than leaning into the discomfort of change. In the process, we unconsciously become a little more numb to life. It's as if we are sending a very subtle message to the universe that we are not really interested in being fully engaged in being alive. We need to be mindful of this because, as we know, the universe is listening (and it can't take a joke); rather, it can only say yes to our deepest beliefs and intentions. Any negative habit is simply the creative energy of life seeking fullness of expression, albeit in a misguided manner. In the *Science of Mind* Ernest Holmes writes, "At the root of all habit is one basic thing; the desire to express life.

There is an urge to express in all people, and this urge, operating through the channels of Creative Mind, looses energy into action, and compels the individual to do something. Back of all this desire is the impulse of Spirit to express. In man, this impulse must express at the level of his consciousness. Some express themselves constructively and some destructively."

Often we lack clarity because negative thoughts, repeated over and over, day after day, and year after year, become ingrained in our unconscious mind where they lay below the field of our awareness, slowly taking on a life of their own. This is the fertile soil in which habits can grow into addictions. It does not necessarily have to be in the area of human relationships either. It could be with habits we have formed in our relationships with work, food, pornography, or any other substance or behavior. The areas in our life where habit energy can assume a life of its own are legion. Regardless of where it shows up in our lives, the energy that drives most negative habits and addictions is the need to avoid dealing with how we really feel about ourselves and life in the present moment. As an example: While some people may feel as dead in their job as my friend does in his relationship, in a strange way, it is safe and comfortable living in the security of conditions that don't demand change, growth, or risk in the present moment. The rut offers fertile soil for habit energy to covertly establish itself in its many subtle ways. Again, a rut is a grave with no ends.

> Whatever your present situation, I assure you that you are not your habits. You can replace old patterns of self-defeating behavior with new patterns, new habits of effectiveness, happiness, and trust-based relationships.
>
> —Stephen Covey

As already stated, negative habits, unchallenged, can appear to take on lives of their own; so much so that some people become enmeshed with their habit energy to a degree they lose themselves in it, and their habits (and addictions) begin to define who they think they are. The first step in changing this is to understand that we are not our habits. Our habits, like our thoughts, are pulsations of energy moving through us. As we depersonalize our habits and see them as energy being directed in a specific way, we can then choose to redirect that energy differently by means of our conscious intention. Habits are a part of the human condition. It's natural to have them. As long as we occupy a human skin, habit energy will seek to have an active role in our lives. So, wisdom dictates that we learn not just to live with habit energy, but to use it to our advantage.

It's important to remember that the current self-image

we are projecting onto the screen of life represents the sum of our belief system, or consciousness. However many years of age we are, that's how long it took to build our consciousness. It is foolish to think we can change overnight a consciousness that took thirty, forty, fifty, or even eighty years to shape. It takes time to reshape our beliefs. I mention this because if we don't see instantaneous results with the effort to change our habits, we need not be discouraged. In the words of Thomas Troward, "Our repeated failure to fully act as we would wish must not discourage us. It is the sincere intention that is the essential thing, and this will in time release us from the bondage of habits which at present seem almost insurmountable." (The power of our intentions will be more fully explored in a subsequent chapter.)

Energy of any kind is neither good nor bad until we direct it in a manner that makes it so. If we are fully conscious of its presence, we can choose to see habit energy as a friend rather than a foe. Begin by ceasing to see habits as good or bad, but simply energy that is being directed (for the most part unconsciously) in one of two ways: constructively or destructively. Once conscious of this fact, we are at choice. Metaphorically, we can choose to be dragged through life by the horse of our habit energy, or we can train that same horse and ride *it*, letting it assist us in moving in the direction of our choosing. A life worth living is built on the positive use of our habit energy. Grooming good habits may require a bit more time and work than do bad habits, but they are a lot more rewarding in the long run, especially if *we* are to ride *them* down the pathway of uncertainty and into the mystery of that which is yet to be.

POINTS TO PONDER & PERSONALIZE

- Can you identify with the metaphor of habit energy being a horse? If so, can you identify areas in your life where your habit energy is pulling you in a direction that doesn't serve your needs in a healthy way? Are you willing to ride your habit energy horse up and out of the rut, even if it means riding directly into the mystery of uncertainty?

- Your needs are always being served, and habit energy is one of your mind's greatest servants in fulfilling those needs, even in its self-destructiveness. In her classic book, *You Can Heal Your Life*, Louise Hay writes, "For every habit we have, for every experience we go through over and over, for every pattern we repeat, there is a *need within us* for it. The need corresponds to some belief we have. If there were not a need, we wouldn't have it, do it, or be it. There is something within us that needs the fat, the poor relationships, the failures, the cigarettes, the anger, the poverty, the abuse, or whatever there is that's a problem for us." Typically, these needs will not be easy to spot because they have been well-camouflaged by years of behavior that has become second nature. Can you pinpoint some of the "unseen needs" embedded in your beliefs behind any current habit energy that may be pulling you in a direction you no longer want to go?

- It has been said that habits carve out a path used to run from pain and, as you know, when used often enough paths can become ruts. Getting out of the rut may require some deep self-inquiry. Knowing that a negative habit is often an attempt to avoid feeling the pain from which you are running, would you be willing to challenge that habit long enough to understand the pain that drives it? If so, are you willing to come to the edge of uncertainty and embrace the effort required to make the needed changes?

- There are a number of things you can do to challenge your habit energy. However, before you can do any of them, you must be conscious and courageous enough to look into the mirror and acknowledge the fact that unconscious habit energy has had its way long enough. You may be led to seek support from a qualified therapist or a specialist in the area where your habit energy is "running amok." The key is to make a decision and act upon it before you again surrender to the habit.

- Remember, a habit, in and of itself, is neither good or bad. It is only energy you have utilized either consciously or unconsciously to a point where it no longer requires your intentional direction. What will determine the quality of the habit is whether it is motivated by inspiration or desperation. World champion runner and Olympian Jim Ryun said, "Motivation is what gets you started. Habit is what keeps you going." When you are motivated to honor the creative urge within to expand in ways that make life a more rewarding experience, good habits become the energizing factor that keeps you going, even when you aren't consciously thinking about it. Get inspired to find new, creative, and joyful ways to harness your habit energy . . . and ride it well.

MINDFULNESS PRACTICES

Before you can challenge and ultimately modify any habit pattern, you must first recognize its presence and make friends with it. In his book, *The Heart of the Bud-*

dha's Teaching, Thich Nhat Hanh writes, "We need the energy of mindfulness to recognize and be present with our habit energy in order to stop this course of destruction. With mindfulness, we have the capacity to recognize the habit energy every time it manifests. 'Hello, my habit energy, I know you are there!' If we just smile to it, it will lose much of its strength. Mindfulness is the energy that allows us to recognize our habit energy and prevent it from dominating us."

Mindfulness is the practice of "remembering to remember" to be present in the moment with what is. When you are fully present you can then become the witness to your habit energy in action. Try it by following this deductive process:

1. As you become conscious that the behavior in which you are currently engaged is driven by habit energy, check in with your emotions.
   - What are you feeling and where in your body are you experiencing that feeling? What feeling is pushing out, trying to get your attention?
   - Just sit with it for a while and observe it. Try not to judge it or find fault with it. Just see it as energy looking for a place to be expressed.

- After you become comfortable with just being with that habit energy, ask yourself what thoughts you were having just before the habit energy began to move toward a specific action. Again, just sit with the idea of examining the thoughts you were having, without judging them.
- Finally, ask yourself: "What beliefs do I have about myself that shaped the thoughts that stirred the feelings that triggered this habit energy behavior?"

2. Through this mindfulness practice you will be led back to the source of your behavior, which will always be your beliefs. In *The Science of Mind, Ernest* Holmes wrote, "That which thought has done, thought can undo. Lifelong habits of wrong thinking can be consciously and deliberately neutralized, and an entirely new order of mental and emotional reaction established in mind. Merely to abstain from wrong thinking is not enough; there must be active right thinking."

- As you continually challenge your habit energy, and learn from it, you will draw more of your authentic power back from it. And, at the same time, you will be given the opportunity to introduce new beliefs about yourself based on "right thinking" that, in turn, can become new life-affirming habits.

- Be patient . . . remember you didn't create your habits overnight and they will not shift overnight. But with time and intention, they *will* change.

3. This is the point at which you begin to ask yourself, "What *positive* habit would I like to put in place of this negative habit?"

- Consider the belief needed to stimulate the thoughts that stir the feelings that motivate the desired behavior, and repeat it until your habit energy kicks in and it takes on a life of its own.
- Remember, what thought has done, thought can undo. In the words of Marcus Aurelius, "Your mind will be like its habitual thoughts; for the soul becomes dyed with the color of its thoughts. Soak it then in such trains of thoughts as, for example: Where life is possible at all, a right life is possible."

Embrace these ideas and put them to work by mindfully remembering that you ride the horse of your habit energy. Choose to ride in the direction of the life you wish to create— one belief, one thought, one feeling, and one habit at a time.

8.

ARE YOU COMMITTED OR JUST INTERESTED?

The Power of the 3 P's

⚜

To truly embody our deepest potential as human beings we have to be more than slightly interested in creating a life of wholeness—we must understand the deeper meaning of commitment. There is no area of our lives that is not radically affected by our ability to be 100% committed; this includes our health, relationships, careers, beliefs and goals. True commitment takes us far beyond the point of no return, and that is where authentic transformation awaits us.

—DR. MIKE WILLIS

Regardless of which area of our life we are called to walk the pathway of uncertainty, we may be assured that commitment, perseverance, persistence, and passion are signposts along the way that will help guide us on the

journey. Be it with desires concerning our health, physical fitness, diet, career, relationships, or other interests,
without deep commitment and the tenacity to move forward into the unknown, the tendency will be to stop
short of our goal and set up camp, settling for less than
what in our heart we know we want and deserve. The
pathway to the top of the mountain is lined with campsites along the way, occupied by those who yielded to the
resistance of walking the path of uncertainty and who
weren't able to embody the deeper meaning of commitment to going the distance. The real question is, are we
committed or just interested in doing the work required
to get us to the top? This is an important question to ask
ourselves because being just "interested" will not get us
there. True commitment will take us past the point of
no return, which is where the mystery of that which is
yet to be holds unparalleled rewards.

I have a neighbor who recently asked me if I was interested in taking a hike through the open hills area
behind our homes. It was a perfect day to walk and be
present in nature, so I said yes. About twenty minutes
into our "hike" he began scaling the steep side of a huge
rock embedded in the wall of the canyon as tall as a four-
story building. Needless to say, since I get dizzy on the
top rung of a six-foot ladder, this did not fit my vision of
a hike "through" the hills. His intention was to go over

this rock rather than through the canyons surrounding it. He egged me on, saying, "You will not believe the view from the top . . . and we can sit up there and meditate for a while." Well, that hooked my attention, so up I went. Two-thirds of the way, I made the mistake of looking down and told him I was rapidly losing my "interest" in the adventure. He shouted down to me, "But now you are more than halfway there so, whether you like it or not, you are really committed . . . *You* can do this!" His cheerleading made the difference, and eventually I made it to the top. He was correct; the view of the canyon below was stunning. Amazingly enough, there was also a gentle path leading down the backside of the rock with a waterfall that I would have never seen had I not gone the distance. Go figure: I got the view, the victory, and a graceful exit strategy to boot. Following my path of uncertainty with commitment indeed had its reward.

> There are only two mistakes one can make along the road to truth; not going all the way, and not starting.
>
> —BUDDHA

Later, while reflecting on my "mountain climbing" adventure, I had an overwhelming sense of gratitude for having made the commitment to go on the hike, but even more so for going beyond the edge of my comfort zone and going the distance. I gained immense confidence from that experience. By looking ahead to the unknown with determination, rather than fearfully focusing on what lay behind me, I truly had a transformational moment that opened a portal through which I had a chance to see my world with entirely new eyes. The awareness I had is that this wasn't just about the spectacular view of the canyon below. It was about how I viewed myself for having gone the distance; that is, I had transcended my own built-in limitations. That is the power to be found in commitment coupled with a willingness to come to the edge of uncertainty. It changes how you view life, but more importantly, it changes how you view *yourself.*

> There's a difference between interest and commitment. When you're interested in doing something, you do it only when circumstances permit. When you're committed to something, you accept no excuses, only results.
>
> —ART TUROCK

Bodhidharma said, "All know the way; few actually walk it." Many of us know what we want and are "interested" in elevating our current view (or experience) of ourselves, someone, or something, but few of us are truly committed to the process unless it's convenient and effortless. As we venture into the land of uncertainty, it's easy enough to come up with a litany of excuses why we can't, shouldn't, or don't go the distance. The reasons we hold back are legion, but all equally effective in keeping us from living our dreams. The most powerful aspect about being 100 percent committed to anything is that it sends a signal to the universe that we are serious about being in the place where authentic power reveals itself in the human condition. The universe conspires to support us when our commitment takes us beyond the point of no return, and the point of no return always opens the door to the mystery of what lies ahead on the pathway of uncertainty . . . to that which is yet to be.

COMMITMENT LIFTS YOU
ABOVE THE NO-ZONE-LAYER

Until one is committed, there is hesitancy, the chance to draw back, always ineffectiveness. Concerning all acts of initiative (and creation), there is one elementary truth, the ignorance of which kills countless ideas and splendid plans: that the moment one definitely commits oneself, then Providence moves too. All sorts of things occur to help one that would never otherwise have occurred. A whole stream of events issues from the decision, raising in one's favor all manner of unforeseen incidents and meetings and material assistance, which no man could have dreamed would have come his way. Whatever you can do or dream you can, begin it. Boldness has genius, power and magic in it. Begin it now."

—GOETHE

We already know the universe always says "Yes" to that which we commit at the deepest level of our being. Goethe's statement above is spot on: The decision that establishes a definite commitment really marks the beginning of a shift in consciousness. From this commitment the most "unforeseen" of beneficent circumstances come our way. This is good news for those who walk the pathway of uncertainty, but it should be of no surprise to us— it's how the Law of Cause and Effect works. We know we don't have to control or manipulate the universe because It knows far better than we how to bring our deepest desire to us when we first do our part. One of the primary things required of us is commitment and, make no mistake about it, commitment comes at a price. We must pay the price of staying conscious and fully engaged in life irrespective of what we are doing or where we intend on going. This is not always an easy thing to do because it is not the way of the world.

Expelled from individual consciousness by the rush
of change, history finds its revenge by stamping the
collective unconsciousness with habits and values.

—ARTHUR M. SCHLESINGER

There is a strong pull by the collective unconscious
to be lulled back from a higher state of consciousness,
where living with commitment is SOP (standard operating procedure), into the habit energy of the masses
where resignation, ambivalence, negativity, and laziness
run rampant. Ernest Holmes referred to this mind-set
as "mental torpor." Torpor is defined as, "a state of mental or physical inactivity or insensibility, lethargy, com-
placency, or apathy." If you consider the energy that
shapes the words in that definition, you'll find none of
them used in conjunction with any definition of commitment. Through my own experience, having personally
lived in "Camp Unconscious" for a number of years, I
have referred to this torpor as the "no-zone-layer," which
is that level of consciousness just above sleep where nothing much is happening other than an unconscious zom-
bielike perfunctory movement through the day, day in
and day out. There is *no* growth and *no* creative expression. In short, there is *no* joy in the *no*-zone. Those stuck
in the no-zone are held there in part by their habit

energy and have not a clue of the unforetold opportunities that lie ahead in the mystery of that which is yet to be.

Unfortunately, much of society exists in the no-zone because it requires so little effort and, as we know, without effort there can be no commitment. To transcend the no-zone-layer requires being fully awake and connected to life in the moment, thriving in each new day, knowing who you are, and knowing that what you do with who you are matters to you and the world. Transcending the wasteland between the no-zone-layer and a commitment-based life is a process that requires clarifying your intention, getting your bearings, and then taking action. With sincere commitment comes focus, purpose, passion, and clear direction. The universe is simply waiting for a sign from you that declares that you are ready to do your part. That sign reads, "Commitment happens here." The practice, then, is to keep on keeping on in the direction that calls you to the higher ground of your being, remembering that true commitment takes you *above* the no-zone . . . *beyond* the point of no return and into the mystery of uncertainty where you'll find no campsites— what you will find are boundless opportunities to create a life worth living you would have otherwise never discovered.

THE POWER OF THE 3 P'S

Persistence, Perseverance, and Passion

Nothing in this world can take the place of persistence. Talent will not; nothing is more common than
unsuccessful people with talent. Genius will not; un-
rewarded genius is almost a proverb. Education will
not; the world is full of educated derelicts. Persistence and determination alone are omnipotent. The
slogan "press on" has solved and always will solve the
problems of the human race.

—CALVIN COOLIDGE

I am by no means a football aficionado. However, I
know a great game when I see one. On February 1, 2009,
the Super Bowl XLIII game between the Steelers and the
Cardinals was the sort of match that fans were hoping to
see. Viewed by 98.7 million people, it was the second
most watched Super Bowl game in history. The decision
as to which team would ultimately win was a "mystery,"
as the game came down to the final thirty seconds of the
last quarter, and it was a real nail biter. In the words of
ESPN.com reporter Greg Garber:

What can you say about a game in which the longest play in Super Bowl history—a 100-yard interception return for a touchdown by Pittsburgh linebacker James Harrison—was almost rendered a mere footnote? A contest that virtually eclipsed the highly anticipated glory-days halftime set of Bruce Springsteen? For more than three quarters, Super Bowl XLIII was idling along toward yet another Pittsburgh Steelers victory when, well, all hell broke loose. When it was over, it may well have been the most exciting Super Bowl ever. Just when it looked like the Arizona Cardinals had authored the greatest comeback in Super Bowl history—scoring 16 unanswered points in the fourth quarter—the Steelers answered with a monstrous, improbable drive.

> Thankfully, perseverance is a good substitute for talent.
>
> —STEVE MARTIN

While Super Bowl fan opinions may vary depending on their team loyalty, I had no favorite player or team so it is easy for me to say the following with no bias: I believe when players reach the level of extraordinary talent that was self-evident in both teams, the game ceases being solely about talent and it becomes as much about heart, persistence, perseverance, passion, and sheer tenacity. There can be no doubt that in their peak moments these guys truly love what they do. The passion oozes though their pores. In short, the team with the most talent did not necessarily win the Super Bowl. The team with the most heart, passion, perseverance, persistence, and tenacity won.

> That which we persist in doing becomes easier for us to do; not that the nature of the thing itself is changed, but that our power to do is increased.
>
> —RALPH WALDO EMERSON

Such is the case with you and me. While we may or may not be athletes, we are all still players in the game called life. Each time you enter the arena with passion, as Emerson infers, you gain more power. Every time you "suit up" and go to work, you are in the game. Each thing you do for your family or others is your contribution to a team effort. Every day when you do whatever it is you do to honor your chosen pathway, you are in the game and, as with the Super Bowl game, how the game will go is really unknown. The question is, beyond your natural talent, your training, and learned knowledge in the fundamentals of how to play the game, is there heart and passion in your game? Do you love what you do? Perhaps most importantly, on those days when you feel

like throwing in the towel, does persistence, perseverance, and determination kick in to get you through?
Don't think for a minute that these qualities won't have
an influence on the field of uncertainty.

While most people consider persistence and perseverance to mean essentially the same thing, they are actually
two sides of the same coin, but each with a separate purpose. Persistence means repeatedly sticking to a specific
course of *action* until you see the results. Perseverance
means sticking to a specific *belief, goal, strategy, vision, or
idea* with deep felt intention. When we combine the two
words, we can witness the energy of our intention to
evolve, moving us toward our vision of a life worth living. In other words, perseverance (our intention) is the
steady application of persistence (our action) toward realizing our purpose, in spite of difficulties, obstacles, or
discouragement. With perseverance and persistence fully
engaged in the moment it will make coming to the edge
of uncertainty a far less intimidating opponent.

> Tough times never last, but tough people do.
>
> —ROBERT H. SCHULLER

We all know these are particularly tough times for the
vast majority of people, not just in our country but
around the world. Many people are facing uncertainty

in monumental ways. Between an ailing world economy and a world consumed in multiple wars, it's easy to get caught in the vortex of negativity that runs rampant in the collective unconscious, and it can influence our predominate attitude about life. It was 1932, in the height of the Great Depression, when Calvin Coolidge declared, "Persistence and determination alone are omnipotent." In essence, he was saying persistence and determination are all powerful, that beyond all other possible fields of influence, it is the altitude of our attitude that ultimately lifts us into a transcendent consciousness that opens the portals through which our personal victories in life are realized. When we add perseverance and passion into the mix, we know we have a great game going. The game I am talking about is never about competing with others. It's about living up to the full potential within us that came as an inherent part of our being when we were born. This "potential" is nothing less than the very essence of universal Presence seeking to take individuated form in our life in ways that fulfill our purpose for being. The important thing to remember is that potential is nothing until it is first recognized in its unformed state, and then actualized on the field of play, which is where the unknown always lies waiting for us to get in the game where anything is possible. Our everyday life *is* the playing field.

Energy and persistence conquer all things.

—BENJAMIN FRANKLIN

This seems to be how the universe works as well: Living things that persist both thrive and fulfill their potential; living things that don't persist just sort of endure and survive, merely getting by until it's time to die, but never really "living." If you look to nature, it's easy to see the energy of persistence at work. Take a look at the weeds in your flowerbed—yes, the same ones you thought you "defeated" last month when you pulled them out; or witness a blade of grass growing through a crack in the concrete. That is the energy of persistence at work. When it comes to human beings, we can add the quality of perseverance, which embodies passion and a conscious goal as well. As an example, watch a five-year-old child who weighs all of 35 pounds gain yet another victory over Mom, getting his way (using the same passion and tenacity a 280-pound fullback uses to get what he wants) by activating the power of persistence *and* perseverance.

> The most difficult thing is the decision to act, the rest is merely tenacity. The fears are paper tigers. You can do anything you decide to do. You can act to change and control your life; and the procedure, the process is its own reward.
>
> —AMELIA EARHART

The same power that fired up the Steelers in those final few seconds of the game and hurled them to victory in that "Super Bowl moment of uncertainty" is available to you the very moment you decide to take action and get into the game with abandonment. It is your commitment to living with persistence, perseverance, determination, and passion for the game of life that lights the fuse that, in turn, ignites the power. If you are feeling the pull of the unfilled potential that awaits you in the mystery of uncertainty, may you consider this your call to action.

POINTS TO PONDER & PERSONALIZE

• Understanding and mastering the power of commitment is vital because there is not an area of your life that will not be positively served by your ability to make conscious commitment part of your daily lifestyle. Your ability to commit and go the distance affects your relationships with family and friends, your work ethic, core values, your physical body, and your material and financial life—commitment is a mighty power to bring with you into the mystery of that which is yet to be. In short, your ability to make and honor your commitments is a declaration to the universe of your character—it says who you are and what your stand for, now . . . and tomorrow.

• Many people make commitments on a regular basis, but they don't always do so well going the distance with those commitments. At the end of the day, it's about remembering that the power of persistence, persistence, and passion is waiting for you to call it forward. It's also about being true to yourself and honoring your word. If making and honoring commitments were that easy, everybody would be living deeply committed, fulfilled, and rewarding lives. Most often, that isn't the case. Keeping your commitments is not always easy, but it is possible. The key to making and honoring your commitments is to stay conscious and engaged in life in the moment, remembering you are part of something significantly bigger than you.

• Do you ever find yourself stuck in the no-zone-layer? Similar to negative habit energy, the mind-set in the no-zone-layer is more about staying numb, surviving, and getting by one more day—living by default, rather than by conscious choice. Our society has created many effective tools that will keep you in the no-zone-layer. As an example, it is a fact that the average American watches over five hours of television every day.

That equals nearly *one-third* of their waking hours. How much of your day do you spend in front of the TV? Overindulging in alcohol, drugs, food, and other habitual behavior is another way to avoid honoring the commitments you make. These behaviors also help avoid any discomfort you may have with the idea of living with uncertainty. These are important issues to explore because becoming aware that you may be stuck in the no-zone is the first step to transcending its gravitational pull—humankind's collective consciousness that is, in fact, really quite unconscious. Remember, keeping the commitments you make only happens when you are conscious.

- Considering the example of the Super Bowl game, can you see yourself as a player in the game of your life? Perhaps your "opponent" is the uncertainty of a difficult job market, a shrinking bank account, a relationship challenge, a physical malady, or (fill in the blank) _____. Can you see that beyond any good luck, fortunate breaks, or your talent, intellectual skills, and special training, it is your passion, persistence, and perseverance that will be a major factor in moving you across the goal line? Are you ready to get in the game? The universe is on your side and it is cheering you on.

MINDFULNESS PRACTICES

If you are to continue moving forward on the pathway of uncertainty, there are, and always shall be, countless areas in your life where obstacles will stand between you and what you want. In his bestselling book, *The Last Lecture,* Randy Pausch wrote, "The brick walls are not there to keep us out. The brick walls are there to give us a chance to show how badly we want something . . . the brick walls are there to stop the people who don't want it badly enough." How badly do you want what lies on the other side of the brick wall? This mindfulness practice will help you see that commitment, persistence, perseverance, and passion is what will get you over, under, around, or even through the brick wall of uncertainty.

1. Write a list of the things (or circumstances) you most desire in your life, but have yet to fully manifest. If you need a place to start, consider some of these issues: New relationships (or improved relationships), a rewarding and satisfying career, prosperity, improved physical and emotional health, deepened spirituality, a more healthy diet, an increased exercise program, more free time, creative expression, and so on.

2. After you have your list, consider each thing that you have written and, one at a time, sit with each one for a few minutes. (If you have a long list you may want to do this over several days.) Ask yourself this question: "Am I truly committed to manifesting this dream?" Listen to your heart and you'll know in an instant. If the answer is "no," cross it off the list because it will only distract you. (Not to worry, you can always add it back to the list later if it is still important enough.) Continue this process with the other things you have written until you get a "yes" answer to your question of commitment.

3. With each "yes" answer, place that thing or circumstance in your mind's eye. Imagine there is a brick wall between you and that thing or circumstance. How does it feel to know that what you most want is, metaphorically, but a few feet away? Can you get in touch with what the joy of reaching that goal would feel like? Just imagine what the Pittsburgh Steelers were feeling the moment they scored those final points only yards from the goal line during the final thirty "uncertain seconds" of the Super Bowl game. Lock onto your deepest feelings of joy and embody that energy.

THE ART OF UNCERTAINTY

4. Finally, imagine how you would feel if you had the courage, strength, and ability to literally jump over that brick wall. If it appears too high, imagine yourself with a shovel, or bulldozer if needed, and begin to dig under that brick wall; if it's too deep, imagine walking around it; if it's too long, see yourself driving your bulldozer through that wall—you are unstoppable. The point is to get in touch with what persistence, perseverance, and passion feel like in action. Also note that you have moved beyond the obstacle of uncertainty. Lock onto those feelings and remember them. This is the driving energy behind commitment.

The key to this visualization is to ultimately bring those feelings into real time with whatever it is you have written down and go to work by putting one foot in front of the other. (It's called action.) Don't fool yourself into believing you may not get knocked down a few times along the way because you most likely will. To this end, I quote an ancient Japanese proverb: "Fall seven times, stand up eight." Press on, indeed.

9.

PATIENCE IS FAR MORE
THAN A VIRTUE

By the Inch, Life Is a Cinch

The key to everything is patience. You get the chicken by hatching the egg, not by smashing it.

—ARNOLD H. GLASOW

A martial arts student went to his master teacher and said earnestly, "I am devoted to learning your art form. How long will it take me to obtain the highest degree black belt?" The teacher's reply was casual: "Ten years." Impatiently, the student answered, "But I want to master it faster than that. I will work very hard. I will practice with great effort every day, ten or more hours a day, every day, if I have to. How long will it take then?" The teacher thought for a moment and said, "In that case, it will take twenty years."

While I am uncertain of the origin of this parable, the meaning is clear: The process of learning anything new, or moving one's life in a new direction, requires time, discipline, and, perhaps most important, patience. In this chapter we shall explore the role that patience plays in mastering the art of uncertainty and how to live in the mystery of life, fully loving it, one small step at a time.

I relate to the story above because it describes to a tee how I lived the first half of my life. It would be safe to say that, while patience may have been a virtue, it wouldn't be one of mine for many years to come. I was addicted to instant gratification in most areas of my life and, as a result, I suffered. At age twenty-seven, when I discovered the universal and transformational principles taught by New Thought pioneers such as Ernest Holmes, Charles and Myrtle Fillmore, Emma Curtis-Hopkins, Mary Baker Eddy, and their predecessors in the transcendentalist movement, such as Emerson, Thoreau, and other enlightened souls, I could not wait to apply them *all* the first week I began my studies. The concepts I was learning were exciting and promised life-changing results to the dedicated student. And believe me, my life was in desperate need of change. I had a real fire in the belly for mastering whatever I needed to learn to transform my

life. However, what I ultimately came to understand, metaphorically speaking, is that you can't pour five gallons of
wisdom into a one-gallon container. I also learned that it
takes time and patience to create a larger container—the
container being one's consciousness, or belief system. I
discovered that adding new content to my belief system
also required me to constantly come to the edge of uncertainty, letting go of old beliefs and ideas and making
room for new and foreign concepts. I was learning that
the "mystery of me was yet to be," and unfolding the mystery was a process.

Suffice it to say that, for all of us, the process of moving from where we have been to where we want to be
can be incredibly difficult if, in the process, we seek instant gratification by trying to learn (or grow) faster than
we can embody the learning. We did not create the consciousness that currently defines our life in an eight-week
course. Our consciousness was created over a period of
many years by embracing certain beliefs about ourselves
and the world, and thinking thoughts that supported those
beliefs, redundantly, until they became embedded in our
mind as our truth about life. Likewise, it requires time to
build a new prototype in our consciousness of the life
we desire . . . one new belief at a time. Clearly, "slow and
steady" wins the race to a life worth living, and patience
makes the pathway upon which we travel a more enjoy-

able and rewarding journey, especially as we make our way into the mystery of that which is yet to be.

CONSIDER THE SIDE EFFECTS OF IMPATIENCE

> Patience is something you admire in the driver behind you and scorn in the one ahead.
>
> —MAC MCCLEARY

Before we can master the virtue of patience, we must first understand the point of origin of its antithesis: Impatience. If you are like me, on more than one occasion you have probably uttered the timeless classic prayer, "Dear God, give me patience and give it to me *now*." A lack of patience is an interesting dynamic because, in part, it deals with many of the core elements that we have come into this incarnation to learn to transcend, such as a need to control everyone and everything. Impatience triggers our attachment to the belief that a clock runs our life. A lack of patience is what separates us from our body. It projects our thinking mind beyond where our physical body is at any given moment. Perhaps most importantly, impatience induces judgment and intolerance of other people's behavior (and abilities) as well as our own. Like many other areas of our life where we find a sense of restriction and limited freedom, impatience draws its life force from fear of "not enough." In this case, it is the fear of not enough time and not enough control over events in our life.

Impatience is the unformed energy of fear looking for a place to manifest, and it is a revealing chain of cause and effect to witness. By means of our consciousness, we are energy directors. It begins with a belief, which triggers a thought, which stimulates an emotion, which erupts as words, which justifies behavior, which then, like a heat-seeking missile, finds a suitable target upon which to project itself. Energy flows freely through all areas of our lives, including our minds and bodies, as well as the body of our affairs. The "target" can be another person, often one of those whom we love the most (including our pets), who is not performing up to our expectations. The target could even be an inanimate object such as a traffic light seemingly stuck on red, or a lawn mower that will not start. When we stop to consider it, the list could be quite lengthy. There is probably no area of your life, or mine, where impatience doesn't raise its snarly little head from time to time. Ultimately, while our impatience may be a source of irritation to others, when our "missiles are aimed" at another person, or the situation at hand, it is we who are the real recipients of the negative effects of our impatience. Why? Because it is we who suffer from the stress and the toxins that get dumped into our body by our lack of willingness to practice patience. Worse yet are the times we become the target of *our own* impatience; for example, when our bodies don't work as efficiently as we want them to or we are simply having a bad hair day. Look how we beat ourselves up with unkind thoughts and words that come from the energy of impatience. Arriving at this awareness allows us to open ourselves to the possibilities of a life of wholeness beginning with the simple practice of being patient. The key is to transcend our egoic, thinking mind. To see this flawless "principle of patience" in action, we need look no further than nature, where we shall find no ego or judgment whatsoever. What we do find is the mystery of Life, simply unfolding, being what It is, in every sacred second, one second at a time.

PATIENCE IS THE PORTAL TO PRESENCE IN THE PRESENT MOMENT

Adopt the pace of nature: her secret is patience.

—RALPH WALDO EMERSON

In turning to nature, we witness the wisdom of patience working at every level. As an example, sit in a garden and allow the plants to be your teacher. You'll never hear a rosebush grunt and strain, trying to force its buds to open. There is wisdom within the rose that knows when it's time to unfold. Likewise, we can't force ourselves to grow faster than we should, any more than we can force a rose to blossom. However, we can have faith that the same Life force that opens the rosebud at the perfect time is also operating through us, and that It knows when to open us as well. Epictetus wrote, "No great thing is created suddenly, any more than a bunch of grapes or a fig. If you tell me that you desire a fig, I answer that there must be time. Let it first blossom, then bear fruit, then ripen." With patience we, too, can ripen naturally. We can learn to pace ourselves, understanding that growth of any kind requires a cycle of the seasons, each with its own rhythm and purpose; some are seasons of light, others darkness. Some of the seasons we must go through are, no doubt, darker than others. The wisdom of uncertainty works in our favor in these times by encouraging us to slow down and move even more mindfully, which requires a deeper understanding and application of patience. Again, learning to witness the mystery of Life as it unfolds is a wise practice. If we can do this one thing we are well on our way to becoming masters of the art of uncertainty.

> Man's task in life is to give birth to himself,
> to become what he potentially is.
>
> —ERICH FROMM

With enough patience, we can learn to trust that we live in a universe that holds unlimited potential for us and is guiding us to that potential 24/7. The only way we can receive that guidance is to open ourselves to it by being present *in the moment* and listening to Infinite Intelligence—the same Intelligence that gives birth to new stars, planets, galaxies, babies, and roses. That Intelligence is waiting to help us give birth to a new idea of what makes life worth living. Clearly, we have a role to play in bringing that idea to fruition. As with any birthing process, there is first a gestation period, and it's comforting to remember that Infinite Intelligence knows the perfect rhythm and timing for that process. Our job is to align with Divine Presence and patiently stay the course, remaining conscious, taking action when guided, knowing in faith that Life always knows how to sustain itself, in us, through us, and as us with grace and ease when we do our part. If we are willing to be consciously present in each moment, it invites us to learn something new. Every time we learn something new we have stepped out of the box of the known and into the mystery of uncertainty. Every person, event, and circumstance offers us a lesson that will enrich our lives if we are open, teachable, and have the patience to mindfully "be" in the process, one step at a time. This is how we give birth to a new expanded consciousness, or perhaps better said, a new idea of who we came here to be. With patience we become the conscious midwife to our own future.

LIFE BY THE INCH . . .

> The Japanese philosophy of kaizen emphasizes that life and business get better a little bit at a time. Progress is made in small, seemingly insignificant increments. This outlook can help any individual or company who wants to move forward . . . Taking very small steps helps you to keep forging ahead and gives you a sense that you are doing something positive.
>
> —Dr. Barton Goldsmith

When I first read the above quote by my friend, Barton Goldsmith, I had a flashback to my childhood when, on countless occasions, I heard my dad say, "Yard by yard, life is hard, but by the inch, life's a cinch." I grew up with that reminder and, as an adult, it has served me in countless ways as I slowly began to understand the meaning behind those words: Patience is far more than a virtue, it is a way of life.

Out of curiosity, I called my dad and asked him where he first heard that saying. As it turns out, in 1957, as an account executive for a major advertising agency, he found himself sitting in the office of the president of the board of directors of the Coca-Cola company. And there it was, on a placard on the president's desk: "By the yard, life is hard, but by the inch, life's a cinch." Perhaps he knew that he was practicing the Japanese philosophy of kaizen.

Now, many years later, my dad, who has created an amazing life for himself and his family, still applies that simple philosophy every day of his life, and it's easy to understand why: If the president of one the world's largest and most successful corporations embraced the "life by the inch" philosophy, perhaps there is something in it for each of us as well. In hindsight, as I look back at how my dad has lived his life, I can see how this philosophy has affected so much of what he has done, in addition to contributing to his mental and physical vitality as he enters his ninetieth year on the planet. I remember as a kid watching him as he slowly, and with great patience, planted and nurtured his roses, gardenias, and avocado and orange trees. He never rushed just to get the job finished. It was as if it was a mindfulness practice for him and he delighted in the process. To this day I can recall the slow, meticulous, intentional methodology with which he would do even the smallest of chores, such as coiling the garden hose, in the same way that he would do larger tasks like painting the house. With the same ease and grace, he also demonstrated unbelievable patience in raising and training a number of Arabian horses, not to mention four "highly spirited" children. There is little doubt in my mind that he observed and learned about patience through his contact with, and love of, nature. I only wish I had understood at a younger age how to apply his wisdom of "life by the inch" in my own life. It would have saved me a great deal of suffering in the early years. Mastering the art of uncertainty is the practicing of patience every sacred second of every minute of every day. The good news is that it's never too late to learn.

SLOW AND STEADY WINS THE RACE

> The road to success leads through the valley of humility, and the path is up the ladder of patience and across the wide barren plains of perseverance. As yet, no shortcut has been discovered.
>
> —JOSEPH. J. LAMB

There is no shortcut to the fulfillment of a life worth living, and sometimes it requires great patience and perseverance, as well as humility, to take the small steps necessary when the temptation for instant gratification is compelling. This is why there is so much wisdom in the saying, "slow and steady wins the race." This sentiment from Aesop's fable about the tortoise and the hare is a metaphor we all understand: It's not the speed, flashiness, or intensity with which we approach any of our desired goals, it's our commitment to be consistent, persistent, and patient—with the clear intention to arrive at our destination—that gets us there.

The world around us may not want to wait for us, but essentially the wisdom of "life by the inch" means slowing down and being present in the moment with a willingness to see what it is offering us and what we can bring to it. Whether we relate to "life by the inch" as folk wisdom, or as kaizen, it seems that when we mindfully do what is ours to do in the moment at hand, the next moment seems to take care of itself. Likewise, when we get to that moment, the next one seems to unfold in a similar manner. It's when we project our attention too far out in front of us that we tend to stumble and misuse (or simply miss) the moment at hand because the mind and the body are in two different places. This can only lead to confusion and, if we are trying to create, accomplish, or learn something new, great frustration as well. Learning patience is a foundational element in mastering the art of uncertainty because it keeps us from trying to stare too far down the road ahead, where the mystery of that which is yet to be awaits our arrival.

> The keys to patience are acceptance and faith. Accept things as they are, and look realistically at the world around you. Have faith in yourself and in the direction you have chosen.
>
> —RALPH MARSTON

Do you ever find yourself projecting your mind too far down the pathway of uncertainty, perhaps driven by fear or worry? I once read that in ancient biblical days people would strap small clay lamps upon their feet at night that would light the way as they walked along the uneven and stony pathways. The lamps would only cast light several feet in front of the person walking, which is really all they needed to move toward their destination, one step at a time. It only required that they pay attention to the next step on the journey, having faith that each step to follow would take care of itself. Perhaps this is what the psalmist David was referring to in Psalms 119:105, when he wrote, "A lamp unto my feet is your word, a light to my path." His awareness of God's presence (Light) in the moment, assured him that each step along the way was guided and that was all he needed to know. As a more contemporary example of how moving forward in the darkness with faith works, consider this the next time you drive your car at night on a dark highway. Your headlights only allow you to see what lies a few feet in front of you, but you still move forward trusting that you'll arrive at your destination miles away by following the light from your headlamps. Now *that* is faith in the mystery of that which is yet to be.

> Everything has its wonders, even darkness and silence, and I learn, whatever state I may be in, therein to be content.
>
> —HELEN KELLER

When we can walk through our days and, metaphorically, our darkest nights, with "foot lamp" faith, patiently taking one small step at a time, we may encounter wonders along the way we never would have had if we were in our running shoes. When we move incrementally, with patience, life gets a little better *and* easier with each step because we can see all that needs to be seen, and we know we are moving in the right direction even when we can't see the final destination. To successfully move forward on the pathway of uncertainty, having patience is not optional. Patience *is* the portal to what is next. By the inch, indeed. Patience is far more than just a virtue. It is the way.

POINTS TO PONDER & PERSONALIZE

* Can you relate to the story about the martial arts student? Do you see any of yourself in his impatience, wanting to learn or grow faster than what is realistic? The telecommunications industry has capitalized on our lack of patience as a culture. We live in a world where nearly everything is instantaneous, from the boundless information available through the Internet to the food we eat, we want it *now*. The seduction of instant gratification causes us to speed everything up, rather than slow things down, and in the process patience gets thrown under the bus. Recent studies show that teenagers with cell phones send an average of ninety text messages a day. Perhaps the idea of waiting until they can call or, better yet, talk in person, never crosses their mind. There is much truth to be found in Paul Sweeney's statement, "How can a society that exists on instant mashed potatoes, packaged cake mixes, frozen dinners, and instant cameras teach patience to its young?" Can you pinpoint any areas of your life where you seek instant gratification, wanting it all *now* and, if so, what will you do about it? Remember, regardless of your age, it's never too soon or too late to slow down and enjoy the journey.

• When driving your car, is your mind ever way out in front of your body? Do you tend to want to move faster than the rest of the traffic is moving and, if so, how does that make you feel? When you are stopped unexpectedly by a traffic jam, red light, or a train crossing, how does that make you feel? While waiting in line at the post office, grocery store, and so on, and the line isn't moving at a pace that satisfies you, how does that make you feel? Where is your mind in relationship to your body? When the behavior of others (including your pets) pushes your impatience button, how does that make you feel? When an inanimate object, such as your computer, isn't running as well as you think it should, how does that make you feel? Finally, what if you, yourself, are not functioning as well as you think you should on a given day; how does that make you feel? As you begin to become emotionally aware and actually experience your feelings and witness your mind, you will begin to become conscious of your impatience and how it causes you to suffer. Awareness is always the first step to disarming the guided missiles of your impatience.

• If you could see your life as being lived in different seasons of light and darkness, what season are you in now? Are you feeling impatient in the season through which you are moving? When you look to nature can you see the wisdom of patience at work and can you see the same Infinite Intelligence at work within you? Can you trust that, with patience, you will arrive where you are going at the appropriate time? As with the practice of kaizen, taking small, incremental steps will move you forward, getting you to your destination with grace and ease. Remember, patience is the portal to peace in the present moment, and the present moment is the doorway to the mystery of that which is yet to be.

MINDFULNESS PRACTICES

There is great power in developing a deeper understanding and application of patience. With patience comes the ability to slow down your mind enough to become the conscious observer of your behavior in the moment. With mindfulness you can witness your impatience and choose to lovingly transform it into patience.

1. Become the observer of your mind and body. Be hypersensitive to those moments when you, or peo-

ple around you, trigger those heat-seeking missiles of impatience, judgment, intolerance, and a need to be in control. You can stop the missile launch by remembering to remember that you live in a spiritual universe and that wherever you are, so too, is the presence of the Infinite One. That remembrance will cause you to slow down and be mindfully present in the Presence. In that awareness, you will not only treat yourself and others with reverence, kindness, and compassion, you'll also realize how much of your power you have given to the clock.

2. Be mindful to notice whether you are at ease or if there is a sense of stress attached to whatever you are doing in any given moment. Spend time outside each day and simply observe nature. Witness the effortlessness in which Life patiently unfolds right before your eyes. Look and listen for signs in nature of forced effort and struggle; you will notice none. Then, align with that Energy of ease and see how it can filter into your life experience each day.

3. If you are in a season of darkness in which you feel an urgency to get through, or you are faced with over-

whelming obstacles, deadlines, and projects or perhaps just the goal of making it through one more day,
this would be a good practice to consider:

- Stop whatever you are doing for a moment and
  take a deep breath. Practice mindful, intentional
  breathing. Consciously breathing in and out slowly
  is a great way to anchor yourself in your body in
  the present moment.

- Then, invoke an awareness of Spirit's presence as
  light, right where you are, by imagining you have
  two beautiful radiant lamps attached to your feet.
  Lift your eyes off of the horizon called tomorrow,
  look down and take just one small step in faith,
  accepting what is, doing that which is yours to do
  in the moment, and trusting the process.

4. Practice patience mindfully. Keep the faith . . . keep
   it simple . . . keep on keeping on, one small step, one
   conscious breath at a time, and you will move closer
   to the life of which you have been dreaming.

10

SETTING THE ALTITUDE OF YOUR ATTITUDE

What Type of Mystic Are You?

The longer I live, the more I realize the impact of attitude on life. Attitude to me is more important than facts. It is more important than the past, than education, than money, than circumstances, than failures, than success, than what other people think or say or do. It is more important than appearance, gift, or skill. It will make or break a company . . . a church . . . a home. The remarkable thing is we have a choice every day regarding the attitude we will embrace for that day. We cannot change our past. . . . [W]e cannot change the fact that people will act in a certain way. We cannot change the inevitable. The only thing we can do is play on the one string we have, and that is our attitude. I am convinced that life is 10 percent what happens to me and 90 percent how I react to it. And so it is with you. . . . [W]e are in charge of our attitudes.

—CHARLES SWINDOLL

In mastering the art of uncertainty, there is probably no subject more vital to faithfully stepping into the mystery of the unknown than your attitude. Your attitude is a deciding factor regarding what is yet to be. Metaphorically speaking, the pathway of uncertainty meets with a fork in the road; one path leads to the gates of heaven, the other to the gates of hell. Heaven and hell are not physical locations, but rather they are states of mind. Which would you prefer to live in? Your attitude will determine which path you will follow.

WHERE IT ALL BEGINS

Your attitude originates in your mind and is formed by your predominant thoughts and beliefs about life and yourself repeated habitually until they become second nature. Then, by means of your emotional body, it filters through your feeling nature and sublimates in your physical body as an energy that permeates every cell, tissue, bone, muscle, artery, organ, and limb. Your attitude colors the lens of your perspective, and literally determines not only how you see the world, but how the world will see you. Your attitude broadcasts an energy

that goes before you to announce your coming. It in-
forms people who you are and what your true values are
even before one word departs your lips. Others can see
your attitude on your face and in your body language,
not to mention your actions. As Emerson said, "Who
you are speaks so loudly I can't hear what you're saying."

Attitudes are forerunners of conditions.

—Eric Butterworth

Consider this: As you come to the edge of whatever uncertainty may look like for you, your current attitude
will play a large role in determining the "conditions" you
will bring with you into the creative zone of the unknown. Because all thought is in essence creative energy,
your attitude is really an energy director sending information (correct or erroneous) to your physical body as
well as the ethereal body of your relationships. In other
words, the altitude of your attitude can affect how well
your physical body feels and functions and, most definitely, how well your relationships with others function.
Another way to say it would be that you are always becoming cause to your own effect, or as the ancients might
say it, "As within, so without . . . As above, so below . . .
It is done unto you as you believe . . . As a person thinks,

so they are," and so on. My point is, a healthy attitude about life and yourself is generally self-evident in a healthy body. Healthy relationships, likewise, are formed and sustained by a healthy attitude. If the condition of your physical body, or the body of your affairs, is less than what you would like it to be, perhaps some self-inquiry regarding the altitude of your attitude is in order *before* you step to the edge of uncertainty. If you are already on the edge looking over, now would be a great time to check in with yourself by reading this chapter as if it was written especially for you.

> Nothing determines who we will become so much
> as those things we choose to ignore.
>
> —SANDOR McNAB

Throughout my years of teaching spiritual principles and mentoring, I have witnessed how even the slightest shift in one's attitude can alter the entire course of one's life in significant ways. Depending on the altitude of your attitude, "significant" can either be the good news or the bad news. Ultimately, your attitude determines how you interface with life. It is your constant companion every moment of every day but, oddly enough, most often you are not even aware that it is operating, let alone *how* it is operating. Monitoring your attitude on a regular basis will assist you in reaching your destination even, if in the moment, you are uncertain in which direction you are headed. During the space race and the return of the Apollo astronauts from the moon in the late 1960s, I remember hearing a leading scientist say that if they hadn't consistently made very small adjustments in their attitude (meaning the spacecraft's direction relative to the earth's position) as slight as one or two degrees on their compass they would have missed the earth by thousands of miles. (This gives a whole new meaning to the importance of one's attitude when moving forward in uncertainty.) The operative word here is *consistently*. That is what this chapter is about. I invite you to think of this chapter as a tool that will assist you in staying consistently on course as you move into the mystery of the unknown by learning how to be conscious, mindful, and vigilant in making ever-so-small *daily* adjustments that determine the altitude of your attitude about life. Thomas Jefferson wrote, "Nothing can stop the man with the right mental attitude from achieving his goal; nothing on earth can help the man with the wrong mental attitude." Achieving a life worth living is more than possible . . . it is inevitable. With the right mental attitude you are *unstoppable*, and it starts by learning how to manage the dynamics of your attitude with conscious optimism.

WHAT TYPE OF MYSTIC ARE YOU?

> Two men look out the same prison bars; one sees
> mud and the other stars.
>
> —FREDERICK LANGBRIDGE

As has been stated numerous times throughout this book,
your perspective plays a major role in how confidently you
will move forward into the unknown, where the mystery
of life awaits you; a healthy perspective on life will make
it easier to trust where the path may lead. How you tend
to "see" life can have a lot to do with shaping your attitude. You are always forecasting your own future, whether
you know it or not. Have you ever considered yourself a
mystic? It has been said all people are mystics, and they
fall in to one of two categories: A "pessi-mystic," who
tends to see the glass as half empty, and an "opti-mystic,"
who sees it as half full. Which are you? I know it's a rather
silly play on words, but I bet you get the point. Irrespective of whether you are an optimist or a pessimist, the
Universal Law of Attraction assures you are predicting
your own future based upon where you are putting your
attention. This is a wise point to remember when we are
called to come to the edge of uncertainty. Your perspective matters.

The universe doesn't know or care if our glass is half empty or half full; that is a determination we make. However, an attitude of gratitude automatically brings with it a shift in consciousness, which says, "I am open to receiving with a grateful heart." With that perspective, life has no alternative but to rush in and fill the glass with good.

—From *The Art of Being: 101 Ways to Practice Purpose in Your Life*

While it may be very dated, the "half-empty or half-full glass" metaphor accurately depicts the filter through which many of us tend to see life. For a great number of people, the past few years have been fraught with uncertainties, disappointments, and fears beyond their wildest imagination. In times like these it's quite easy to allow ourselves to go unconscious and fall prey to the purveyors of gloom and doom who are peddling their latest version of how empty the glass is. The pessimist usually buys what they are selling because it validates his view and gives him permission to continue to stare at what's wrong with life. On the other hand, the optimist isn't even in the market because his attention is gratefully on what is right with life.

> Become a possibilitarian. No matter how dark things seem to be or actually are, raise your sights and see possibilities—always see them, for they're always there.
>
>   —NORMAN VINCENT PEALE

Which type of mystic are you? Do you view whatever lies between where you currently are and where you would like to be through the eyes of an opti-mystic or a pessi-mystic? The altitude of your attitude determines not only what you see, but your experience of it as well. In Zen, there is an old saying: "The obstacle is the path." A person with a well-balanced attitude knows that a whole and happy life is not free of obstacles. He knows that, if anything, a whole and happy life comes with an abundance of obstacles. However, what he is also infinitely aware of is that those obstacles can also be seen as the perfect stepping-stones that will lead him to higher ground, where he will have a new and unobstructed perspective of what lies directly ahead on the pathway of uncertainty. Indeed, what kind of mystic do you choose to be? Choose wisely because your future happiness is being determined by that choice. Regardless of whether one is pushed by pain or pulled by inspiration, a "possibilitarian" will come to the edge of uncertainty knowing that only good lies ahead—and of course the universe has already agreed.

ARE YOU WAITING FOR HAPPINESS TO HAPPEN?

> The man who makes everything that leads to happiness depend upon himself, and not upon other men, has adopted the very best plan for living happily.
>
> —PLATO

Regardless of what has called you to the edge of uncertainty, to a large degree, what allows you to live in the mystery and love it is the attitude you choose to bring with you. Maintaining an affirmative, uplifting attitude literally shapes your unseen future with positive light, and at the same time brings purpose, meaning, and, perhaps most importantly, happiness to whatever you are doing in the moment regardless of where you may be— and I mean that literally.

As I sat preparing to go into meditation, I gazed out the window of my room on the twenty-eighth floor of the Venetian Hotel, appreciating the unparalleled view, when suddenly a man appeared right in front of me on a scaffold and began washing the window. As if that weren't enough, he was also happily singing what sounded a lot like, "What a Wonderful World" at the top of his lungs as he listened to his iPod. My initial reaction was, "Oh, great! I can't meditate with this guy just hanging there, singing like the leader of a Las Vegas karaoke band, looking directly at me as if I was his audience." Then, I noticed the window was so darkly tinted that he couldn't see me at all. He wasn't putting on a show for me. This guy was genuinely happy doing his job, and I was being invited to anonymously bear witness to the attitude he brought with him to that job. That was when I realized that my master teacher for the day had just descended from above and was dangling, suspended right in front of me, as if sent directly by God.

> I am still determined to be cheerful and happy, in whatever situation I may be; the greater part of our happiness or misery depends upon our dispositions, and not upon our circumstances.
>
> —MARTHA WASHINGTON

I must admit I woke up that morning feeling less than joyfully connected to life, and then this fellow dropped in and began giving me a personal concert twenty-eight stories off the ground in 105-degree desert heat. In my estimation, he didn't seem to let the extreme conditions of his work environment determine his state of happiness. I couldn't help but smile in appreciation of his attitude. Since heights are not my favorite place to "hang out," I could no sooner do his job than I could walk on a tightrope across the Grand Canyon. But the one thing I witnessed that day was someone who loved what he was doing, and it was revealed by his attitude. It gave me pause to consider the attitude I sometimes bring with me to my work.

> There is little difference in people, but that little difference makes a big difference. The little difference is attitude. The big difference is whether it is positive or negative.
>
> —W. CLEMENT STONE

I have often said that the altitude of our attitude has everything to do with our state of happiness, but I never expected to see it played out in such literal detail. At times, I have wondered if happiness is the cause of a positive attitude, or if a positive attitude is the cause of happiness. I suppose it doesn't really matter as long as we are clear that, in either case, it is an attitude that finds its point of origin within us. Spiritually speaking, happiness is a derivative of joy, which is what we feel welling up from within the core of our being in any moment when we are completely aligned with, plugged into, turned on to, and tuned into "Life" (which is another word for the presence of Spirit), which can happen anytime, anywhere, because it is not reliant upon external conditions. Next to love, joy is the essence of the Divine in Its highest vibration. Happiness is the horn by means of which authentic joy trumpets Spirit's presence in the human condition, and it really is an inside job. That was the teaching I received that day: Happiness is not based on what's going on "out there." It's based on what's going on within our minds and hearts—an important lesson to remember when standing on the precipice of uncertainty.

> Most folks are about as happy as they make up their minds to be.
>
> —ABRAHAM LINCOLN

The lesson my window-washing guru brought to me is simple, but not always easy to practice if our tendency is to look to the world for our happiness. The idea that we bring happiness with us wherever we go is not the way most human beings are conditioned to think because we have been taught that happiness is a condition at which we arrive when everything is as it "should be." That's why so many people seem to be so unhappy. They are waiting for happiness to pull into the station like a train that may or may not stop to pick them up. If it stops, life is good in that moment; if it passes them by, life is not so good. Like any attitude, happiness is not something that comes to us; it happens *through* us when we consciously choose to make space for it to do so. For the window washer, "Happiness Happens" hanging twenty-eight stories off the ground because he brings it with him. How about you? How much happiness will happen in your life today? In other words, how much happiness will you bring with you the next time you walk out the door of your home or, for that matter, in that door? Don't fool yourself into believing that by leaving a job, or relationship, or city, because you are not happy there, you'll suddenly find it in the next job, relationship, or city. Remember, wherever you go, there you are; you will not find happiness there waiting for you on your journey into the mystery of uncertainty—you must bring it with you. Choose to make a space to let happiness happen through you regardless of where you may be. Who knows, you may even feel like singing, "What a Wonderful World." Perhaps now would be the perfect time to pause to consider the fact that you have been given another precious day of life on this planet. That simple awareness, alone, will cause the altitude of your attitude to soar in a heartbeat.

POINTS TO PONDER & PERSONALIZE

• Remember that your core beliefs mold your attitude about life. They shape your attitude about politics, religion, and people, including any prejudices, preferences, and opinions you may hold regarding others. The practice with this awareness is to be conscious enough to witness and challenge those parts of your beliefs that don't serve you and your world in beneficent ways. Your attitude is simply the projecting device that allows you to see what you really believe. Challenging the beliefs that no longer serve you is the first step in altering the altitude of your attitude. What attitude about life will you carry with you through the doorway of your home and into the mystery of what each day brings?

• Be mindful of the fact that, via your reactive mind, your attitude can also be influenced by what is going on in the world around you. The media, current events, the opinions of others, and, perhaps more so, the *behavior* of others can greatly influence your attitude; that is, until you become fully conscious and responsible for what shapes your attitude, which is *your* current belief system and thinking. As you become more mindful of how the collective unconscious can influence your thinking, you can literally "stand guard at the temple gate" (your mind) and choose what ideas and beliefs to let in. In the words of Emerson, "Your own mind is a sacred enclosure into which nothing harmful can enter except by your permission."

- Can you relate to the idea that your attitude directly affects the health of your physical body and the body of your relationships? How you manage your energy system in the future will depend largely upon the altitude of your attitude today; your future literally depends on it. Are you more of an opti-mystic or pessi-mystic when it comes to your own well-being? If you are standing on the edge of uncertainty today in either of these regards, it's never too late to change your attitude. Would you rather take an optimist or a pessimist with you on your journey into the mystery of that which is yet to be? That is what you must do—it's your choice.

- Because you are a spiritual being as well as a human being, there is a place within that knows how to take you through the portal of uncertainty with grace and ease. As mentioned in a previous chapter, there lies within you an inherent intelligence, an "onboard guidance system" far more capable than any computer pro-

gram NASA could ever develop. It knows how to guide
you through life on a course of trajectory that is stun-
ningly accurate, and it is completely available to you
24/7. However, like the Apollo astronauts, you have a
role to play. This is why your willingness and ability
to monitor the altitude of your attitude is crucial. You
have to continually be vigilant of your actions in any
given moment. This is done by becoming the conscious observer of your mind, thoughts, feelings, words,
and behavior, understanding that if you find yourself
drifting "off course," you can make the needed adjustments in your attitude, trusting that the infinite intelligence that put you on this journey in the first place
knows how to do the rest.

- What lesson about happiness and attitude did you learn
from my window-washing guru? Have you been waiting for happiness to show up in your life? Thich Nhat
Hanh wrote, "The present moment is filled with joy
and happiness. If you are attentive, you will see it." Are
you able to see that the present moment is where happiness has been patiently waiting for *you* to show up?
Are you willing to let go of whatever you have been
clinging to so that happiness may happen in you and
through you now? Remembering that joy is the energy
of the Divine seeking expression, are you willing to

be the instrument through which it flows? It's as easy as being present in the moment and realizing that your oneness with God is already a given fact that is never subject to conditions. Happiness is a choice you make, and it finds its home in your daily attitude about life when you invite it to.

MINDFULNESS PRACTICES

As you have discovered, your attitude is like a launching pad that hurls you headfirst into life each day, pointing you in a certain direction. It determines what kind of day and, ultimately, what kind of life you shall have. You now know that attitude is more important than facts or conditions, and you are "at choice" every day regarding the altitude of the attitude at which you shall fly that day. In other words, you are in charge. These mindfulness practices will assist you in being conscious of the altitude at which your attitude is functioning.

1. Can you see yourself as what Norman Vincent Peale referred to as a "possibilitarian"? Is your attitude one

that allows you to look directly into "what is" and, regardless of how dark it appears, see the light present there? As an attitude adjuster, stand outside tonight and gaze into the darkness of space and focus on only the void between the stars. Then, slowly allow your eyes to focus only on the light of one star. How does it feel to see the light of that one star in the midst of all that darkness? Lock into that feeling and remember, with the right attitude you will train yourself to naturally look for the light, not the darkness, on your pathway into the mystery of the unknown.

2. As a litmus test to determine how in touch you are with the true altitude of your attitude, in your mind's eye think of your attitude about life as a movie projector broadcasting your core beliefs onto a movie screen you can see. Be honest with yourself, and write on a piece of paper what you see. Then, imagine that you are not alone and there are other people in the theater viewing the same screen. Do they see the same thing you do? The way to find out is to ask three people you trust and respect to give you their honest feedback regarding what you have written. Make it safe for them to give you their honest response and, if

necessary, be prepared to elevate the altitude of your attitude, one new thought at a time.

3. Do you consider yourself to be an opti-mystic or a pessi-mystic? One of the quickest ways to become an "opti-mystic" is to begin a mindfulness practice that focuses on building an attitude of gratitude, taking time to focus on what is right with your life. William A. Ward wrote, "God gave you a gift of 86,400 seconds today. Have you used one to say, 'Thank you'?" Here is a mindfulness practice that will require a bit of commitment, but the result will be self-evident in your attitude:

Create a Mindfulness Journal
- Begin a Mindfulness Journal and maintain it for the next thirty days. Each day list three things (from the tangible to the intangible) for which you are grateful.
- At the beginning of each subsequent day begin by reading what you have written from Day 1 of your journal and then add three new things to the list for the current day. (Do not put the same thing down twice.)

You will discover that at the end of thirty days you will have deeply seated within your consciousness the good already existing in your life and the seeds for new and expanded good in your future. This is the attitude you will want going before you to announce "your coming" as you continue your journey into the mystery of life. Are you loving it yet?

NOTE

You can download a free thirty-day Mindfulness Journal as my gift to you directly from my Web site: www.DennisMerrittJones.com. Click on the Press Room link and scroll to "Free Downloads."

II.

ABUNDANCE IS THE GIFT ALREADY GIVEN

How Big Is Your Bucket?

⚜

Abundance is not something we acquire.
It is something we tune into.

—WAYNE DYER

The intention of this book is to focus our attention on what is required to come to the edge of our uncertainty and step with confidence into the mystery of that which is yet to be. In no small way, this requires our understanding of the universal principle of abundance. Though they are two very separate concepts, many people confuse abundance with prosperity. Abundance is a supply of more than enough of whatever you can possibly conceive of, while prosperity is a demonstration of that supply in the material world. There is already a preponderance of self-help "prosperity" books available today about how to get more "stuff," so that is not the intention of this chapter. Instead, this chapter is about exploring the universal principle of abundance with the understanding that it is not something you can gain or lose, own, buy, trade, or sell, but rather that it is an unseen field of energy. As Wayne Dyer implied, abundance is a principle you align with and, in so doing, allow to serve you. As you align with it, you convert its energy into that which you can see, i.e., prosperity. Because it is an omnipresent universal principle and not a material thing, you don't have to take abundance with you on your journey into the mystery of the unknown; wherever the pathway of uncertainty may lead you, the principle of abundance is already there waiting for you to tune into it. In short, there is more than enough, and even more waiting within the mystery of that which you cannot see with your physical eyes today. As you deepen your understanding of the principle of abundance and its availability to you, it will make the edge of uncertainty a much more comfortable place to be, especially if you have to live there for any extended time.

> Man was born to be rich, or grow rich by use of his faculties, by the union of thought with nature.
>
> —RALPH WALDO EMERSON

We don't have to look too far to confirm that we live in a prolific and abundant universe. We need only to look to the sky or nature to see a demonstration of abundance as a universal principle. In his book *Abundance Is Your Right*, Arthur Thomas writes, "The Sun could contain one million planets the size of our earth. . . . Expansion of the known gives contact with stars that are large enough to hold five hundred million Suns. . . . [T]he average galaxy contains one hundred billion stars, while known space holds at least one hundred million galaxies. The galaxy to which our earth belongs comprises one hundred thousand million stars, with new stars forming. . . . It is an expanding galaxy in an expanding universe which knows nothing about limitation or shortage."

> The source is within you,
> And this whole world is springing up from it.
> The source is full,
> And its waters are ever-flowing.
> Do not grieve; drink your fill.
> Don't think it will ever run dry, this endless ocean.
>
> —RUMI

The universe is expanding at the speed of light, and you and I are part of that expansion. The message the universe is sending us is that there is more than enough. The principle of abundance makes it clear there is no shortage of anything good in the universe; the only lack appears to be our lack of understanding of how to access that good and *keep it flowing.* Developing a natural sense of abundance will open the floodgates of our good. Abundance is the gift already given; we don't have to earn it. Prosperity is the demonstration that we have accepted the gift. The first step to "tuning into" the principle of abundance is to establish a consciousness that is based on an awareness of your oneness with the universe, with Life—the Source and Supply of it all. In his classic book *This Thing Called You*, Ernest Holmes writes, "You belong to the universe in which you live, you are one with the Creative Genius back of this vast array of ceaseless motion, this original flow of life. You are as much a part of it as the sun, the earth and the air. There is something in you telling you this—like a voice echoing from some mountain top of inward vision, like a light whose origin no man has seen, like an impulse welling up from an invisible source." That very impulse rushes before us to announce our coming—it's there before we are. Isn't it comforting to know that in whatever area of your life you may be forced to come to the edge of uncertainty and step into the mystery of that which is yet to be, the principle of abundance awaits your arrival? The next question is: "How much of the unlimited good available to you are you prepared to accept when you arrive?"

WHAT DETERMINES THE
SIZE OF YOUR BUCKET?

The well of Providence is deep. It's the buckets we
bring to it that are small.

—MARY WEBB

If we are observant, we can see how the ups and downs
of the stock market have been affecting people's sense of
well-being. For many, the Dow is like a barometer that
dictates how we should be feeling each day. When the
Dow is up, we have a tendency to feel good. When
the Dow is down, our tendency is to feel a bit down and
a bit uneasy as well. My sense is that most of us are more
worried about the well running dry than about the size
of the bucket we're taking to the well. Here is the good
news: From a perspective of universal abundance, the
well can never run dry because it is Infinite in supply.
Remember, the universe is expanding at the speed of
light—that expansion brings with it an ever-increasing
amount of potential. If there is one thing for absolute
certain, even in the face of the many uncertainties with
which we are all dealing, the universe knows nothing
about "not enough." The challenge, particularly in eco-

nomically difficult times such as these, is that it is easy to be seduced into believing in limitation, and in the process our bucket seems to get smaller every day as we buy into the "drama." The state of the economy has nothing to do with the supply of our good because the economy is not the source of our good. Don't let the drama of the Dow skew your perspective of the availability of abundance.

The principle of universal abundance is composed of *unformed* energy or Infinite Potential until you *give form* to it by means of your consciousness. To illustrate this, visualize going to a well that is rich in resources beyond your dreams, and so deep that you can't even see the bottom. Imagine that this well contains whatever good you seek to be a healthy, happy, fulfilled, and whole person. Now, lower your bucket down deep into the well and, with no effort at all, pull it back up. How much "good" is contained in your bucket? The answer is obvious, isn't it? It all depends on the size of your bucket: A pint-sized bucket can hold only a pint of good, while a five-gallon bucket can hold only five gallons of good. But what if your bucket were the size of a fifty-gallon drum . . . or the size of a swimming pool? How big is your container? Whatever its size may be, that's the amount of good you will have . . . and no more.

The concept of the bucket is a classic metaphor because it's one with which we can all identify. Think of your personal bucket as your consciousness. Your consciousness is shaped by your beliefs, and your beliefs determine the quality *and* quantity of what goes into the bucket. In other words, the bucket represents the level of your prosperity consciousness, which is based on your sense of self-worth, as well as understanding of the principle of abundance and your oneness with it. So, once again, the question is: "What size is your bucket?" If your experience in life isn't yielding enough of whatever you are seeking, don't go searching for another well because there is only one well and it is Infinitely deep. Get a bigger bucket! As you step into the mystery of the unknown, the one known factor you *can* count on is that, regardless of its size, you will bring your bucket with you. Understanding the principle of circulation is a great place to begin to build a bigger bucket.

THE LAW OF GIVING AND RECEIVING ISN'T AN OPTION

Because your body and your mind and the universe are in constant and dynamic exchange, stopping the circulation of energy is like stopping the flow of blood. Whenever blood stops flowing, it begins

> to clot, to coagulate, to stagnate. That is why you
> must give and receive in order to keep wealth and
> affluence—or anything you want in your life—
> circulating in your life.
>
> —DEEPAK CHOPRA

Regardless of where we look in life, we can see the Law
of Giving and Receiving (aka the principle of circulation) in action. Life is energy in motion. Energy must
continue to move to maintain balance and good health
in any form. In the *Science of Mind* Ernest Holmes states,
"Prosperity is the out-picturing of substance in our
affairs . . . we must receive, utilize and extend the gift."
This is a triangular process wherein receiving, using, and
releasing energy is mutually important. Think of the
many different areas where you are in relationship with
life. Consider the give and take relationship you are having at this moment with your physical body, even if you
are not conscious of it: Your body has a digestive system
that receives and gives energy in one form or another on
a continuum, and it knows that in order to stay healthy,
it can never hold onto all of it. You give your body food,
and that food converts to energy. The body willingly
receives the food, releases that which has served its purpose, and transforms the energy of that food into skin,
hair, organs, blood, muscles, fingernails . . . and so goes

the cycle of exchange. If there is a breakdown anywhere in the flow of the energy loop, stagnation and disease set in. The same could be said about your heart as well. In order for it to function properly, it can't pump more blood than it receives. If you are mindful enough to observe this natural process, you will have more confidence in the Infinite Intelligence you cannot see that accompanies you into the mystery of that which is yet to be— It knows better than you how to sustain you.

> The sage never tries to store things up. The more he does for others, the more he has. The more he gives to others, the greater his abundance.
>
> —LAO TZU

The amazing thing is that our body practices circulation with no conscious effort on our part. However, what about the many other areas of life where the Law of Giving and Receiving is still operating flawlessly, but is not always mindfully *practiced*? This is when a different type of "disease" can set in. As an example, in our relationships with other people, it is a draining experience to be with those who only know how to take and not give back. In a manner of speaking, that type of relationship is unhealthy because there is a definite lack of the ease that normally comes in the form of energy moving

in a circular manner. Of course, the biggest breakdown
for most of us is with our relationship with money. Many
of us go totally "comatose" when it comes to our cash
flow. We forget all about the principle of circulation,
which is the same principle that sustains our physical
bodies so well. How often do we tend to squeeze the life
force out of a dollar by trying to hold onto it? Money is
only one form of energy in motion, but it must flow
unrestrictedly in order to serve us and others in life-
affirming ways.

Whether we may come to the edge of uncertainty out
of necessity, or simply the desire to honor the Divine
Urge to push out and create something new, the principle remains the same: If, in either case, we allow fear
of not enough to overtake us, and we begin to crimp
down, we will impede the flow of energy, irrespective
of what form it takes. Circulation is a natural principle,
and we must learn to honor the complete cycle because
that is how abundance manifests in the form of prosperity in every area of our life. The Law of Giving and
Receiving can't work differently in one area of our life
than another. That includes everything from the consideration and respect we give others, to the hugs, smiles,
and time we offer others. The size of our bucket will
determine how much good we are able to give and how

much good we are able to receive. For those of us who perceive our bucket as less than half full, this premise can be challenging and somewhat paradoxical.

Herein lies the paradox: If you want more of whatever it is you desire, you have to first prove to the universe that you are capable of having it by developing a consciousness that affirms there is no shortage of it. The only way to do this is by creating a vacuum or space for it to be received, and the only way you can create a space for it to be received is by letting go of what you do have, trusting that the universe knows what it is doing. That's the law of circulation in action. To people enmeshed in fear of "not enough," this logic will make no sense at all. So they cling and hoard, which simply broadcasts a message to the universe that they lack, to which it responds, "Let me help you prove it." To a person who is established in a conscious awareness of his unity with the source of all good, it can be no clearer. Letting go is a prerequisite for receiving. We can do this more easily when we trust the principle of abundance and the law of circulation.

—From *The Art of Being: 101 Ways to Practice Purpose in Your Life*

RECEIVING IS AS
IMPORTANT AS GIVING

In order for the Law of Giving to work effectively for us, it also requires that we be as *equally* good at *receiving* as we are at *giving*. Being an open and willing receiver is one way that we can support others in fulfilling their own practice of giving. When my daughter, Merritt, was very young, she was constantly bringing me her latest crayon renderings of things that, quite frankly, I could not discern as being a cat or a tree. However, I always made a fuss over how "amazing" they were and excitedly accepted and proudly posted them on the refrigerator or my office wall for all to see. By being a worthy recipient of her gifts when she was at a tender age, I helped her grow with confidence into a creative, joyful, generous giver as an adult; one who knows that the gift she brings to the world is valuable. Clearly, receiving is as important as giving. If we are out of balance in either of these areas, we stifle the life force that seeks not only to sustain us, but allow us to grow and prosper as well. How good are you at receiving? It will be no less important than giving when you are standing on the edge of uncertainty.

Many people have a difficult time receiving from others. This may come from the shame-based, "I am not enough" mind-set. Shame is the original hole in the soul: If we don't feel worthy, how can we be a worthy recipient of any good thing? Perhaps it goes back to the biblical saying, "It is more blessed to give than receive," but taken at face value (and out of context), that is unhealthy advice. Which do you tend to do more of, give or take? To show you the necessity of finding balance between the two, try this: Right now, take a deep breath in and hold it for as long as you can. Conversely, now exhale all the air from your lungs and do not take another breath and see how long you stay conscious. To think that is better to give than to receive is the same as thinking it's better to breathe out, than in. The bottom line is that you have to be willing to both give and receive to stay healthy. Using this analogy, I invite you to explore all the various areas of your life and see where it may be relevant. Life is far too long to live with a hole in your soul that continually drains the joy of being fully alive. If a lack of self-worth is diverting the universal gift of abundance that seeks to flow to you and through you, I encourage you to get the needed support to heal and transcend that issue. The practice of freely giving and receiving will sustain you in unforeseen ways as you travel the pathway of uncertainty. Remember, the omnipresent principle of abundance is already there awaiting you, wherever the mystery of the unknown may lead you.

YOUR WORK IS LOVE MADE VISIBLE

> Always you have been told that work is a curse and
> labor a misfortune. But I say to you that when you
> work you fulfill a part of earth's furthest dream, as-
> signed to you when first that dream was born, and
> in keeping yourself with labor you are in truth lov-
> ing life. Work is love made visible.
>
> —KAHLIL GIBRAN

I have often wondered how many of us have ever thought of our work, as Gibran puts it, as a curse and a labor of misfortune. If we were really in touch with the affect our thinking has on our abundance consciousness, we might be more inclined to think "up" rather than "down." One of the obvious ways we demonstrate our relationship with an abundant universe is through that which we call "our job." When we do our job we are practicing the principle of circulation by exchanging the energy of our time, skill, talent, passion, and physical and mental labor, for a paycheck, which in turn, we then convert to an-other form of energy called money. We then circulate the money by converting it into yet another form of energy called food, gas, electricity, mortgage payments, school clothes, vacations, doctor bills, and so on—and so goes the cycle of giving and receiving, utilizing and extending the energy and gift of life. The question is, do we do our job with joy, gratitude, and love, or perhaps less than that? In either case, as we now know, the altitude of our attitude affects our relationship with the universal principle of abundance accordingly, not only today but even more as we continue our journey into the mystery of that which is yet to be.

I have been blessed with one job or another since I was fourteen years of age, and I suspect many of you reading this book have been equally blessed. For the past several months, I have been spending ten-hour days, sitting at my computer, "working" on this book. Gibran's words truly resonate with my heart. Because I love what I do, I consider this book to be a "labor of love," and I treat it as such: Each day, as I sit down to write, I take time to give thanks for being given the opportunity to do what I do and prosper at it as well. I thank Spirit, which I consider my Muse, for Its guidance and inspiration, and I bless my computer for working in partnership with me. I also bless my fingers, eyes, mind, and "behind" for the role they each play. (I've truly come to believe that the mind can absorb only what the behind can endure.) Finally, I bless every person who will ever pick up this book and read it, knowing that the love and intention imbued in its pages will be felt by that person.

Everyone has been made for some particular work,
and the desire for that work has been put in every
heart.

—RUMI

Someone once said, "Your job is what you do to feed
your body and tend to your physical and material needs,
and your work is what you do to feed your soul (and
humankind's) and tend to your spiritual needs." While
the two may seem mutually exclusive of one another (or
can be) they don't have to be. I like the idea that my job
can also be my work, and the logic of it is quite simple:
When you truly love what you do, you do it *with* love.
From a spiritual perspective, loving what you do transforms your "doing" into "Being." Whenever your soul
and body commingle as one in the present moment, there
is a sacred sublimation of energy that moves through you
and it opens you wide to your creative genius—at which
point you become the vessel or conduit through which
the universe finds expression with grace and ease. As
John Ruskin wrote, "When love and skill work together,
expect a masterpiece." That masterpiece can be your life.
Do you love what you do? If you do, perhaps you can
relate with what I have said. If you don't, I encourage
you to open yourself to the unlimited possibilities that
lie in the field of the unknown, and do some exploring

because life is not *too short*, but rather *too long* not to be doing what you love. You may want to go back and re-read the introduction and first chapter of this book, and perhaps you will read them now through new eyes. It is also possible to love what you do by changing your perspective of what you do. The importance is not so much what you do, but the mindfulness, intention, and reverence with which you do it. This is how your "job" can also become your "work."

If you are among the many who have been affected by the economy and are without a job, you still have *work* to do, and that work is to stay "prayed up," positive, and open to new possibilities. If you are jobless, you stand with many others at the door of great uncertainty. The primary difference is that, by knowing what you now know about the difference between abundance and prosperity, you can also see that door as a portal to new opportunities that have yet to be discovered. Understanding that the principle of abundance applies to jobs, you now know that there isn't so much a shortage of jobs as there is a shortage of creative thinking. Consider opening yourself to the possibilities of a job, perhaps in a field totally unrelated to what you have been doing. Doing so will help you get into the flow.

What will set you apart from others is your understanding of the principle of abundance and your intention to remain unified with it. Keep coming back to the awareness that the source of your good is not a job. Your job is a conduit through which your good can flow. Because there appears to be fewer jobs then there are people to fill them, many of those who understand the principle of abundance are busy reinventing themselves. In the process, they are creating new jobs for themselves through inventive thinking. They are not "waiting" for the world to serve them with another job, they are "serving" themselves. It could require additional work-skill training, or education in an entirely new field. One way or another it may require you to step out of the box, aka your comfort zone. As stated in chapter 1, using the metaphor of the baby birds: There is an intelligence within you that knows how to soar far beyond the confines of your current experience, but you have to be willing to come to the edge and lean into the mystery of uncertainty and take the leap.

As you head out the door to do that which is yours to do, if it is your job, and whether you love it or not, realize how blessed you are. If you are without a job and desire one, affirming your unity with the Source of all good is a great place to start, then be so conscious of Infinite Presence that you bring your Being into whatever you are doing. In this way, all that you do will, indeed, be a labor of love.

POINTS TO PONDER & PERSONALIZE

- As you take a look at how you approach life each day, give some thought as to the size of the bucket you carry with you: Is your bucket the size of a cup or a much larger container? If there is any specific area of your life where there appears to be less than "enough," challenge that appearance—not by complaining that the "well isn't deep enough" to satisfy your needs, but by asking yourself, "Why is my bucket so small?" Listen carefully and you will be given the wisdom needed to build a bigger bucket. Rather than blaming the size of your bucket on the economy, or whoever or whatever you may have been holding responsible for your supply of good, take an unbiased look at your own consciousness. What are your deepest beliefs about your own self-worth . . . about your place in the universe and your ability to be a worthy receiver and a joyous giver of life's energy? It is impossible to operate authentically from an attitude of "there is enough" without first having a foundational underlying belief that "I am enough." What can you do today to deepen your sense of self-worth? This is important work to do as you move forward into the mystery of what is next for you because wherever you go, there you are!

• Take time to explore the intentions that lie behind your desire to accumulate things. Be clear that there is nothing wrong with having lots of "stuff" because stuff is great. However, it is wise to understand the reasons why you want it. Do you own your stuff, or does your stuff own you? Often, obtaining "stuff" can be an unconscious attempt to fill the hole in the soul—that place within where "I am not enough" lingers. The "I am not enough" consciousness is established in a sense of powerlessness. If the hole in the soul is big enough, material things can become a symbol of external power that we mistakenly think will fill the hole. It never does because it can't. Only authentic power will fill the hole in the soul. Self-worth is the bridge to authentic power because it can only be found within. This is also the place where true Self-worth is born.

• Can you relate to the idea that your job is what you do to feed your material needs and your work is what you do to feed your soul's needs? How might you see the universal principle of abundance serving you equally in both? Do you love what you do? If you currently have a job, can you recognize it as a wonderful energy channel through which a portion of your abundance flows, while at the same time understanding that it is not the source of your good? If you currently don't have a job, the same premise holds true: A job is not the source, it is a conduit. Whether you have a job or not, this awareness will set you free to explore new conduits through which your good can come to you. This awareness could open the door to the mystery of the unknown in enchanting and enticing ways. Perhaps your "job" really can become your "work." How might you become the conscious vessel through which an abundant universe brings substance and supply to you and the world? Are you curious and courageous enough to explore that question? Practicing the art of uncertainty will point you in the right direction.

MINDFULNESS PRACTICES

Whether you are thrust onto the ledge of uncertainty through no conscious choice of your own, or you are drawn to it by your desire to expand and grow, the same principle of abundance is at your disposal. Many of the things discussed in this chapter can be difficult to practice if you have been operating from the "I'm not enough/there is not enough" belief system for a majority of your life. These mindfulness practices will assist you in closing the hole in the soul.

1. Since the principle of abundance is "universal" and omnipresent by nature, it applies to every aspect of your life where you desire increase. Where would you like to see a greater demonstration of abundance in your life today? The universal impulse is to expand, and it doesn't differentiate between materiality, abundant health, joyously happy relationships, and other quality of life issues. Can you see the principle of abundance showing up in various and different ways in your daily life?

   • First make a list of those areas where you would like to see a greater flow of abundance.

   • Remembering the key to expansion is through the practice of generously giving and gratefully receiving, next to each thing you have written down, write an action step with a timeline declaring when and how you will prime the pump by giving some portion of that which you are desiring *more of* yourself . . . with no strings attached.

   • A good way to prime the pump of generosity is by starting with the intangibles such as a smile, or a simple courtesy such as opening a door for someone or extending some other random act of kindness. Consider giving time to mentoring a young person, and so on. This might be referred to as *generosity of spirit*.

- Then, when you are well-established in the flow, begin to give material things that are in your comfort zone, such as buying someone else's lunch unexpectedly, bringing flowers to someone you might be visiting, etc.

- Finally, come to the edge of your comfort zone and give of yourself and your possessions in ways that may cause you to step out of that comfort zone. Continue to come back to "I am enough and there is enough" and feel the joy of being generous just because you can be.

- The key to true abundance is to offer the gift of your whole self to others with no expectations or strings attached. When you give with expectations of getting, you taint the gift. Trust that the universe will take care of how and when your opportunity to receive shows up.

2. Set time aside specifically dedicated to uncluttering your home (including your garage) and workplace. In doing so, you will create an opening to receive a greater flow of abundance.

- Clean out your closets and drawers. If you have not used something in over a year, it is not likely you will in the future. Stop waiting for those shoes, dresses, or suits to "come back" in style.
- Clean out your garage and have a yard sale, and as people come to buy what you have set out, witness the principle of circulation in action.
- If you really want to activate the Law of Giving and Receiving, take the money you earn from the garage sale and give it to a nonprofit organization . . . and feel the joy of participating in an abundant universe.

3. If you have not yet begun a Gratitude Journal, this is the time to do so. Entering each day with a grateful heart serves to open you to an even greater flow of abundance. Review the Mindfulness Practices in the chapter titled "Setting the Altitude of Your Attitude" if you would like some guidance in creating your personal Gratitude Journal. Remember, the gift has already been made. Giving thanks is an affirmation; you have accepted the gift!

12

HOW CONSCIOUS ARE
YOUR CHOICES?

*It's Choice, Not Chance, That
Determines Your Destiny*

❧

> Choice is the engine of our evolution. . . . [I]f
> you choose unconsciously, you will evolve un-
> consciously. If you choose consciously, you will
> evolve consciously.
>
> —GARY ZUKAV

Have you ever stopped to consider the number of choices you make daily? This is an important question because the more conscious you are about your choices, the more likely it is you will end up where you want to be at the end of your stay on this planet. Other than the functions of your physical body, which are automatically controlled by your autonomic nervous system, *every* moment of your life is defined by the choices you make. The choices you make today have everything to do with who you shall become in the future as you continue your sojourn on the pathway of uncertainty. Every day you make countless choices, so why not ensure that they are conscious choices? As an example, do you remember everything that you chose to put into your body yesterday? Do you remember when you last thought about (or avoided thinking about) doing your exercise program and the action you chose to take (or chose not to take) to follow through? Those choices affected your physical body. Moreover, do you remember the words that came out of your mouth; meaning, do you recall the manner in which you chose to speak to and treat every person with whom you had contact? Those choices affected the body of your relationships. Do you recall the day you made the choice to go to college or not to, to get additional training to enhance your job skills or not to, to buy or sell a home or not to, to have children or not to, to take or leave a job or not to, or enter or exit a relationship or not to? Every one of those choices affected your life as it is today.

From the seemingly commonplace daily choices you make (mostly unconsciously), to the colossal once-in-a-lifetime choices you make, your choices all have one thing in common: They determine the quality of the life that you shall live. Armed with this information, it becomes obvious that the choices you make today will shape who you shall become tomorrow, and that they will also determine the karmic circumstances that will follow you, like a loyal puppy, into the mystery of that which is yet to be.

> You can run but you cannot hide because making choices is not an option.
>
> —DMJ

Paradoxically speaking, every time you have a choice to make and you don't make it, by default, you are making a choice *not* to make a choice, which is, of course, a choice. You have no choice in the matter <smile>. As odd as it seems, your life functions by choice whether you like it or not. The only choice you have is whether you shall be a conscious participant in the process, or stand on the sidelines and watch your life parade by you day by day, living in a default state of mind where choosing not to make mindful, conscious, intentional choices becomes the norm. When you make conscious choices, the clarity and intent of those choices will determine the direction in which your life is headed. As a rule of thumb, in the span of most people's day, it seems that they live with their "choice meter" set in the default mode, which I refer to as "autopilot." If you want to live an extraordinary (*extra*-ordinary) life based on healthy, life-affirming choices, you can't fly through life on auto-pilot.

As you look at the world today, it may seem that the majority of humankind exists at the level of living a life that is stuck on autopilot, unaware that the choices they make every moment of every day, individually and collectively, determine their experience on the planet. This is self-evident with the mindless damage being done to our environment and ecosystem and, perhaps even more so, through conflict between human beings around the world. For the most part, the choices being made today by the collective whole of humankind are not really being made with consideration for the next seven generations yet to come. When you exist on autopilot, the tendency is to live unconsciously, carelessly, self-servingly, and reactively, rather than proactively. One could say that, as a species, we have made more than a few mindless choices. I find this interesting given the fact that our ability to make conscious choices is one of the primary things that separates us from every other species on earth. The fact is that (irrespective of the degree) every choice you make leads you closer to, or further away from, being the person you desire to be and, likewise, the world you want to pass on to your children's children. The more conscious you are in the choices you make, the clearer you become about who you really are. The more willing you are to make conscious choices, the more opportunities to consciously evolve will be presented to you in the mystery of tomorrow.

TRANSCEND THE FEAR OF MAKING MISTAKES

> The difference between greatness and mediocrity is often how an individual views a mistake.
>
> —NELSON BOSWELL

Too often, we choose to settle for the status quo because of the risk involved with new discoveries. We fear we may make a "mistake" venturing outside our box (current reality) and so we settle in for the long run, living our lives with an inner knowing that there is something greater awaiting us beyond our comfort zone. It woos us, inviting us to move forward into the unknown where anything is possible, including making mistakes . . . so we hold back. The belief is that mistakes are a bad thing. The fact is that a person who has never made a mistake has never tried anything new.

> —From *The Art of Being: 101 Ways to Practice Purpose in Your Life*

How often have you held back on making a choice to move forward with an idea or some action because you were uncertain or feared that in the future it might prove to be a mistake? Any venture that moves you in the direction of your vision of a greater life will require you to accept the fact that making mistakes along the way is a normal part of the process. It's how you perceive them and what you do with them that matters. If you are conscious, even making a choice that mistakenly sends you in the wrong direction on the highway of life can move you toward your goal because you can always choose to make a U-turn.

The forgiving thing about having free will is that when it comes to moving forward on the pathway of uncertainty you can choose and, if that choice isn't the appropriate choice, you can choose again. This is important to remember because when your life is stalled and at a standstill, making *any* choice is often better than making no choice if it gets you moving. (Remember the Universal Imperative, "grow or die.") Consider the idea that when you come to an intersection while driving your car, the choice as to which way you turn can literally determine what happens next in our life. The metaphor is that your life is always at an intersection. You are at an intersection right now; which way is your life inclined to go? When living in the mystery of uncertainty, if you are willing to ask and listen, there is guidance available to you.

TUNING IN TO YOUR DIVINE GPS

> The intuitive mind is a sacred gift and the rational mind is a faithful servant. We have created a society that honors the servant and has forgotten the gift.
>
> —ALBERT EINSTEIN

Too often, we listen to the mindless chatter of the "rational" conscious mind and ignore the deeper wisdom of the intuitive mind. When you were given life and issued the body in which your soul currently traverses the planet, you were blessed with the gift of free will. As part of the deal, you were also gifted with a built-in internal guidance system to help you make choices that guide you to your highest and best good. You might think of this guidance system as "Divine GPS" because it came factory installed by the manufacturer. This internal guidance system knows what you need to know as you move forward into the uncharted territory of uncertainty. Another word for this internal guidance system is intuition. In the animal kingdom, every creature lives and survives by instinct. Instinct is divine guidance working at the level of "animal." At the level of animal, there is no real free will. Instinct will always lead an animal in a direction toward its survival. The same intelligence is working through human beings as intuition, broadcasting its "guidance beam" to all of us 24/7. The primary difference between the animal kingdom and ourselves is that animals don't have an ego to get in the way, and we do. The disadvantage of free will is that we also have the ability to ignore the guidance that is being offered *all* the time. This is paramount information to embody as you navigate your way through the mystery of uncertainty: You are always at choice.

> Back of the conflict of ideas; back of the din of external life and action; back, back in the innermost recesses of uplifted thought and silent contemplation, there is a voice . . . we must learn to listen for this voice. Call it conscience, intuition, or what we will, it is there. No man need go unguided through his life, for all are divine at the center . . .
>
> —ERNEST HOLMES

Life is full of choices and decisions every day. Not a day goes by when you don't have to make life-altering decisions regarding your work, your relationships, your living accommodations, and so on. If you are present in the moment and listening, your intuition will tell you whether you are doing your due diligence in evaluating all the facts you need to consider before making a decision. Remember, your intuition is there to guide you, and to ensure your survival and well-being. As an example: Have you ever been driving your car and been guided, for what seemed at the time "no good reason," to take an alternative route, and after doing so, discovering that there had been an accident or delay of some sort ahead that you had averted? And, on the other hand, have you ever received that same message and ignored it, only to find yourself in an accident or some other delay? Point in fact, you were not willing to hear *and listen* to your Divine GPS. There is not an area of your life where being in tune with your intuition will not serve you well. I have found this to be particularly true when it comes to relationships and business dealings. My inner guidance system will send up red flares warning me if the person (or people) with whom I may be considering an affiliation is (or are) to be approached with trust and ease, or caution. Unfortunately, I've had to learn that one the hard way. Perhaps, you have too. While you may think that common sense "should" prevail, your head may say one thing, but if you are willing to be present and honestly listen to your "gut," you may hear something else; and, in the process, be given clear guidance on what is for your highest and best good.

> Intuition is a spiritual faculty and does not explain,
> but simply points the way.
>
> —FLORENCE SHOVEL SHINN

Following your intuition means that you must really listen to your own internal guidance system—the one you were born with—even if, in those times of uncertainty, you are fearful and the direction leads you down a path you may have never traveled before. Listen to your intuition as to whether any pending course of action is the correct one for you. Listen, and be courageous enough to act in trust and faith, even in the face of that which you might fear the most. To argue or debate with your intuition is fruitless because it uses no words, only feelings. Those feelings will point the way, and no explanation is needed because you'll know . . . that you know . . . that you know.

Is the universe "waiting for you" to listen and follow Its lead? No. Rather, it's similar to having a radio: Is a radio station waiting until you turn on your radio before it broadcasts its signal? If you want to listen to a certain station, you must first intentionally turn on the radio and tune in to that station. Conversely, if you don't want to listen to the radio at all, you can choose not to. In either case, the broadcasting station continues to disseminate its signal. In kind, Infinite Intelligence is always broadcasting; whether you are "tuned in" and receiving its guidance, or not, is the question. The challenge is that even when you are tuned in, divine guidance doesn't necessarily reveal Itself in the form of thunder and lightning bolts, spelling out exact instructions in the sky as to what you should do. This is where emotional awareness comes in. In the process of making choices in the midst of uncertainty, if you are in touch with your body senses, your emotions will help point the way.

As you ponder the choice that lies before you, ask for guidance, and then be mindful of where in your body system you feel an impress of subtle energy. Most often, energy will begin to stir in your solar plexus and then rise to your heart center. You may not hear the guidance in words so much as in a sense of "knowing that you know" without it having to go through the intellect. Often times, your intuition will reveal the guidance you have asked for through a dream, or in a certain passage of a book you may be reading, or perhaps in a conversation you may be having with another person. When you are open to it, the information you seek will find its way to you. The practice is to maintain a sense of connection with the Knower within as part of your regular daily disciplines, and then your intuition will be much easier to access because you have already "dialed into the frequency."

If you are intuitively tuned into the flow of life, you can trust that the guidance being offered in every instant is for the highest and best good, not only for yourself but for everyone else involved as well. In his classic book *This Thing Called You*, Ernest Holmes writes, "Divine Guidance is yours for the asking. The answer to any problem which can ever confront you already exists at the center of your being . . . if you wish to be certain that the impressions that come to you are from Spirit, analyze them and see if they are of the nature of the goodness and peace which Spirit must be. God never sets one man's opinion against that of another. God, being love, never wills hate or destruction. God, being peace, never ordains confusion."

It's important to understand that your "highest and best good" can't be defined as a predetermined event or condition. Never mistake divine guidance for predestination. There is no such thing as predestination. If there were, God (or whatever name you might choose to call It) would be nothing more than a sometimes benevolent, sometimes not so benevolent, judgmental dictator or puppet master, and that's not the case. This does not mean your life unfolds by chance either. In the words of Jean Nidetch, "It is choice—not chance—that determines your destiny." Life has no specific plans for you, other than the karmic energy you bring with you that is always shaped by the choices you make moment to moment. As you begin to make conscious choices, your karma shall follow the trajectory of those choices even as your shadow faithfully follows you wherever you go. Conscious choices allow you to steer your karma, rather than being chased by it. In other words, your highest and best good lies patiently waiting for you to make conscious choices that guide you directly *to it*. Consciously choosing, and then choosing again if necessary, is how we evolve into the beings we came here to be; it has everything to do with our freedom of choice and how we are guided to use it. Remember this always as you walk the pathway of uncertainty—choice is the engine of your evolution.

APPROPRIATE PRIORITIES AND CONSCIOUS CHOICES GO HAND IN HAND

You can have anything, but you can't have everything.

—ERNEST HOLMES

At times what may keep us from moving forward in life is that we have too many options from which to choose, and we get bogged down because we want it all, which, of course, is literally impossible. I recall a time taking my then twelve-year-old grandson, James, shopping for a "hand-picked" birthday gift. As we strolled the aisles of James' favorite store, in a frenzy he began grabbing nearly every item in sight. Sensing the opportunity at hand to be one of those precious grandpa-grandson mentoring moments, I said to James, "You can have any *one* of these things you are so hot for, but you can't have them all, so you'll have to make a choice." Clearly he was not pleased with that caveat. He asked why, and how would he know which toy to choose anyway? I replied that he'd need to learn how to compromise and choose his priorities wisely because when he grew up to be a man he would be faced with many such choices, only the cost of the toys would be different. Then I asked him, "Which toy do you *feel* the most excited about? That is the one you may want to choose. The one you feel the most passionate about is the one you'll enjoy the most." After all that, he chose a set of dueling super-soaker squirt guns, one for him and one for me. I smiled all the way home.

> When it comes to making choices there are those moments when it's as if we are nothing more than kids in big people's bodies.
>
> —DMJ

As adults the issue may not necessarily be about having all the toys we want. However, it generally revolves around wanting *all of something*. Is there an "I want it all" mind-set at work anywhere in your life today? Through the conscious, affirmative, and creative use of your mind, perhaps you really can have just about *anything* you want, but you can't have *everything*. It might mean that to have that specific circumstance or thing you most want, you'll have to let go of certain people, places, or things to which you may be attached. As I shared with my beloved grandson: In application and practice, the skill we may most need to learn is the fine art of compromise, prioritizing and choosing wisely. I know it was not easy for James to let go of some of the things he had in his hands that day, but he did; and, I was proud of him. I believe that action also helped him appreciate more fully the gift he ultimately chose as the thing he cherished most. In other words, the act of letting go of the "I want everything" mind-set placed a greater value on that which he chose as most important to him. What is most important to you today, and what might you need to choose to let go of to have it in your life? Surely, if a twelve-year-old can master this universal premise and promise, so can we. As we move forward into the mystery of that which is yet to be, every step offers us another choice. Choose wisely.

POINTS TO PONDER & PERSONALIZE

• Until now, how conscious have you been of the choices you make on a daily basis? How much of your day do you run on autopilot, living by default, allowing other people, circumstances, and events to make up your mind for you? If you tend to avoid making conscious choices, are you willing to challenge that behavior? As you become witness to your own behavior, observe the times and people with whom you are most prone to flip on the autopilot when it comes to making choices. Notice that, quite often, when you refuse to make conscious choices for yourself, you will attract others who are only too happy to make up your mind for you. Living by default may feel safe because it allows you to avoid responsibility for the choices you would otherwise be making. However, it is not the way to express your personal freedom, purpose, and reason for being on the planet.

• Has the fear of making a mistake held you back from making choices that are needed to move you forward in your life? Remember, making mistakes is not a bad thing, if in the process you learn from the mistake and it moves you off the sidelines and into the game. Once you are in motion, you can choose to reset your compass if necessary. What is most important is not to allow the fear of making mistakes keep you from stepping into the mystery of the unknown, which is where all new creation takes place.

• Remember that you came hardwired with the innate wisdom to make choices that support you in creating a life worth living. Your intuition is available 24/7; you need only be mindful of its presence and make yourself available to its guidance. The universe conspires for your good, but you have a role to play in accessing that good. Empty yourself out, ask for guidance, and listen intently. Don't try to manipulate how it will be revealed to you . . . just remain tuned in, and trust.

• Can you relate to my grandson's dilemma in the toy store? Making conscious choices will support you in keeping your priorities in order. Be sure that your priorities include the highest and best, not just for yourself, but everyone involved. Also, be prepared to let some things go in the process by remembering you can have just about anything in life, but you can't have everything.

MINDFULNESS PRACTICES

How conscious are you with the choices you have been making? The Mindfulness Practices in this chapter are dedicated to assisting you in "remembering to remember" that you are *always* making choices and that every choice you make contributes to shaping your future. Mastering the art of uncertainty and living in the mystery of life becomes a joyous journey when you know you are a conscious participant with Life by means of the choices you make.

1. When it comes to making wise choices, one of the areas in which many people tend to go most "unconscious" the quickest is with what they put into their mouths, which always has a direct affect on their body and mind.

   • Create a journal that you can carry with you for the next week. Make note of everything you eat or drink. This action alone will begin to awaken you to your ability to choose consciously. Your mind wants many things, but your body needs only certain things; the innate wisdom within you knows the difference.

- Before placing food or substance of any type in your mouth ask yourself, "Knowing this will affect my well-being, do I *want* this _____ or do I *need* it?" Listen to your intuition and you'll know the answer. Then make a choice that reflects and honors that guidance.

2. Each day you make hundreds of choices, from simple to life-changing.
   - Witness your feeling nature as you ask yourself these questions: Is the choice I am about to make driven by unconscious habits, fears, doubts, and insecurities, or by love, trust, and optimism knowing that the universe supports me?
   - Awareness of the motivation behind your choices is essential to making conscious choices.
   - As a litmus test to discern how conscious your choices are, pay attention to your emotions, because they won't lie.

3. Often people avoid making tough choices "by default" because they don't want to take responsibility for the choice at hand. Each time they do so, they give away a bit more of their authentic power. On the

other hand, each time they make a conscious choice, they claim a bit more of their authentic power.

- The next time you catch yourself being tempted to flip on the autopilot default switch, ask yourself this question: Is the choice I am faced with at this moment going to create authentic power for me or am I placing my power outside of myself by looking to other people, places, and things for approval, purpose, and direction?
- Listen, and you'll literally know in a heartbeat.

4. Another way that people tend to live by default is by saying, "I can't" when, in truth, it's not really a matter of ability, but choice. This is most often related to their need for approval and fear of rejection, and sometimes just plain laziness.

- As a technique to becoming the conscious witness to your choice of words, place a rubber band (not too tightly) around your wrist. Listen to your words and self-talk for the next few days. When you catch yourself saying, "I can't" when, in actuality, you know in your heart you can, snap the rubber band. Then step into your power, making a choice to use words that reflect the awareness of a conscious evolving being.

- To say, "I choose not to," rather than "I can't," brings an amazing amount of authentic power and freedom with it . . . *and* the welts on your wrist will begin to subside. <smile>

13.

PAY ATTENTION TO
YOUR INTENTION

*Your Vision Is Your Compass
to a Life Worth Living*

⚜

If you don't know where you are going, you might
wind up someplace else.

—YOGI BERRA

A great teacher once said, "I am in this world, but I am not of it." What I believe he meant was that while we may know our current experience is not the ultimate reality of the life we have come to live, we still have to be conscious enough to navigate *through* it. There is an inherent danger of losing our way to a life worth living if we get *too* comfortable in the land of uncertainty; that is, without a sense of intention, uncertainty can become an excuse to loiter, a place to just "hang out" on a journey that ultimately takes us nowhere. Living in the mystery of life does not mean that we can become so disconnected with the relative world that we lose all sense of the direction in which we ultimately want to go.

I invite you to do this visualization with me: Imagine that you have a passionate desire to take a trip from New York to Miami, Florida. You and a traveling companion start your road trip with a good deal of excitement— your car has new tires, a full tank of gas, and you are on the open road; the top is down so you can see all the sights, your favorite music is blaring, the wind is blowing through your hair, and you are on a roll! Hours pass by and as you drive through Chicago, you and your friend are joyfully jabbering away, talking about what a great time you are going to have once you arrive in Miami. You are so excited about being there that you decide not to stop to take pictures as you pass by Lake Michigan. Then, suddenly you realize . . . Chicago . . . Lake Michigan . . .? You never "intended" to go to Chicago. It's not even on the way to Miami, Florida! How did you end up there? "Where did I go wrong?" you ask yourself. The problem arose when you forgot to pay attention to your intention and, in the process, your unbridled passion and desire to "get up and go" carried you further away from your original intention and goal.

> Attention energizes, and intention transforms. Whatever you put your attention on will grow stronger in your life. Whatever you take your attention away from will wither, disintegrate, and disappear. Intention, on the other hand, triggers transformation of energy and information. Intention organizes its own fulfillment.
>
> —DEEPAK CHOPRA

The "road trip" described above is how many of us navigate through life. In order to achieve some specific outcome in life, desire alone is not enough to get us to our destination. We must couple paying attention to our intention. When we fail to do so, it's like having a detailed course to our ultimate destination already punched into the car's GPS and never turning it on because we are so busy looking at the scenery passing by. When we wake up and turn on the GPS, we discover we are further away from our goal than when we started. Training our mind to pay attention is the first step to getting where we want to go. Traveling the pathway of uncertainty requires a delicate balance of faith, passion, intention, *and* attention.

> Your intentions determine the trajectory of your
> life. If you are not aware of them, you follow a path
> that may lead you to places that you do not want
> to go.
>
> —GARY ZUKAV

Often times, the untrained mind can be distracted in another way as well, which is focusing (obsessing) on what's wrong or not working—where we have already been, or where we don't want to go. Paying attention to where we have come from and don't want to go back to is sort of like staring into the rearview mirror as we speed down the highway, rather than paying attention to where we are going. It can be very detrimental to our future plans. Even if on the pathway of uncertainty we don't have all the details about where we are going, with focused attention *in the moment* we can at least channel enough energy to move out of the box in which we may be stuck. Harry Emerson Fosdick wrote, "No horse gets anywhere until he is harnessed. No steam or gas drives anything until it is confined. No Niagara is ever turned into light and power until it is tunneled. No life ever grows great until it is focused, dedicated, disciplined." Our mind is a finely tuned energy director and tracking device: That to which we give our unfettered attention becomes the target of our creative energy. An attentive and disciplined mind can target the intention of a life worth living, create a plan, *and* take us there.

TRAINING YOUR MIND TO PAY ATTENTION IS A PROCESS

> There is nothing so disobedient as an undisciplined mind, and there is nothing so obedient as a disciplined mind.
>
> —BUDDHA

When Mac Doodle (my Labradoodle/Goldendoodle mix, remember him?) was six months old we went through an eight-week basic training obedience course. I really don't think Mac considers himself to be *my* dog, as much as he does me to be *his* human, and that became abundantly clear as "we" began the obedience training. I discovered that I really needed to pay attention to the instructor because *I* was the one being trained, not Mac. Mac was just there to assist me in learning how to be a more focused, present, disciplined, patient, forgiving, loving, spontaneous, playful, and attentive human being. Giving less than my full attention at the classes was not an option because Mac's training would begin each week when we got home from class. Now, I would *like* to say that the communication was two-way and clear from the start, but that would not be accurate. My job was to communicate to him that which I had learned at class; however, to do so, I first needed to get and hold *his* attention. Getting and holding a fifty-five-pound, six-month-old, ultra-high-energy puppy's attention is rather like trying to get the attention of a New York City taxi-cab driver in a blizzard on a Saturday night: The moment of opportunity comes and goes in an instant, and you are left standing there all alone.

At the time we began the training, Mac had an attention span of about five seconds. Because of his short attention span he made quite a mess of things very quickly. At times, he may have been doing something that was, shall we say (at least from my perspective) nonproductive, such as chewing on a shoe or dragging a (previously) potted plant around the house, leaving a trail of dirt, leaves, and puppy paw prints behind him. In those moments, when I would call to him, more often than not, if I didn't hook his attention immediately, he would ignore me completely; the five-second window had opened and closed, and he would just go on making a mess. At first, I took it very personally, as a sign of rejection, and it frustrated me that I couldn't gain and hold his attention. Then, I realized I was competing for his attention with something far more compelling than me: the instant gratification of a nondisciplined puppy mind that simply loved to be entertained by whatever was most available and hooked his attention *in the moment.*

AN UNTRAINED MIND
CAN MAKE A MESS

> One reason so few of us achieve what we truly want is that we never direct our focus; we never concentrate our power.
>
> —TONY ROBBINS

Sometimes our minds are like Mac's mind: nondisciplined and always on the lookout for instant gratification. The gravitational pull of instant gratification can be as compelling to us as it is to Mac. We must be certain not to confuse our desire to live in the mystery of life with an unbridled desire to wander onto the path of instant gratification and diversion. When our minds are not focused and disciplined, it's hard to resist the lure of whatever diversion is most available and first hooks our attention. We all have those moments when we are doing that which is ours to do, when our puppy mind, with its diminished capacity to stay on point, wants to pull us off course. It happens to me quite often when I sit down to write or meditate. (Some meditation teachers might refer to puppy mind as "monkey mind." If you have ever seen a monkey in a confined area, you can understand why the term fits.) Teaching an untrained mind to "sit and stay" is asking it to contain itself in a very confined area and, just like Mac, it will resist. As long as I stand right over Mac and give him the command "Sit and stay," he does stay. However, the moment I turn my back, he is off making another mess. The good news is that the more often I do it, the better he gets at staying. It's just a matter of sticking with it until his "habit energy" kicks in and he associates the words with the action.

The same applies to training the undisciplined mind. An untrained mind will continue to make a mess of our lives the minute we take our attention off of it. A good affirmation you can use to train your mind to stay present is "Be . . . here . . . now." The practice is to keep on keeping on, coming back to the present moment until your mind gets that this is where you want it to "sit and stay" and to focus its attention. There is little difference between training a dog and teaching our mind how to pay attention to our intention: It requires patience, persistence, loving-kindness, discipline, and time. What does all of this have to do with moving forward on the pathway of uncertainty? Allowing the puppy mind to have its way with us is a great way to avoid paying attention to our intention of moving from where we are to where we wish to be.

HAVING A VISION FOR YOUR LIFE SETS YOUR COMPASS OF INTENTION

> To come to be you must have a vision of Being, a Dream, a Purpose, and a Principle. You will become what your vision is.
>
> —Peter Nivio Zarlenga

The mystery of that which is yet to be is always calling to us. One of the best ways to enter that mystery with a sense of peace, confidence, and certainty comes with having a vision for our lives. This kind of vision is not that which comes as a result of using our physical eyes, but rather it comes as the result of our using our hearts and minds. Having a vision for our life is using the "Inner I" to see the possibilities for something wonderful before it is ever manifest. A vision is something that every person, family, business, and organization can and should have. It can act as a compass that moves us forward and determines where we are going and, perhaps more importantly, what we stand for. It clarifies our purpose for being and summarizes our core values and principles.

Many people are so busy just doing life, getting by day to day, that they lose touch with the deeper purpose and meaning of life itself. They wander aimlessly from day to day and, as days turn into years, on the final day of their journey here, they look back and think, "That's it? Where was the juice and sweetness and meaning of being here?" Without a vision, our life's journey can seem meaningless. We tend to blow about like a sailboat on the ocean without a rudder. If we are not committed to intentionally navigating our lives with vision, any current moment "trauma drama" will pull us off course, and we will lose sight of the shoreline—our goals and destination . . . our reason and purpose for being. Conversely, as we clarify our vision, our lives become energized and begin to move in a direction and dimension we haven't seen before. In the words of Ralph Waldo Emerson, "A good intention clothes itself with power." True visionaries are few and far between because living a vision-led life requires a willingness to go where they have not gone before—no doubt this is the call of mystery of the unknown. Of course, that too is where the juice, passion, purpose, meaning, and uncertainty lie waiting for them. It requires the courage and commitment to declare a course and stay with it, irrespective of the sailing conditions that blow others off course so easily.

It takes someone with a vision of the possibilities to attain new levels of experience. Someone with the courage to live his dreams.

—Les Brown

A person who lives a vision-led life is really a self-fulfilling prophet, one who doesn't try to predict his or her future, hoping it will come true if certain conditions prevail, but who is busy creating it by paying close attention to personal intention and following his or her vision. It's about becoming so clear about where we want to go, what we want to be, and what we want to do when we get there that life has absolutely no alternative but to take us there. Note that I didn't mention "how" we are going to get there. The "how" will show up naturally on the journey, but first we need to decide on the "where." That intention alone will open wide the portal of possibilities. Carlos Castaneda wrote, "Learn to see, and then you'll know that there is no end to the new worlds of our vision. . . . In the universe there is an immeasurable, indescribable force that shamans call intent, and absolutely everything that exists in the entire cosmos is attached to intent by a connecting link." That link is the Infinite Intelligence that guides all creation: It holds the stars and planets in place and creates new galaxies while moving at the speed of light; and not only do we have direct access to It, we live *in* It and It lives in us, awaiting our command.

If we have the vision (intention) and the courage to follow that vision, the Universe will do Its part. When we know where we are going and can hold that vision in our mind, we automatically chart a course and the world is ours to circumnavigate. The idea of "knowing where we are going" may sound like a contradiction to the idea of living in the mystery of uncertainty; however, having a clear vision does not determine the course, only the destination. The mystery is the journey itself. Ultimately, we are no different than Christopher Columbus or any of the other ancient explorers: We have to have a clear vision of our ultimate desire, and then leave the safety of the harbor of the known, setting sail into uncharted waters of uncertainty, literally sailing into the mystery of life. Paying attention to our intention is paramount to moving forward on the journey to that which is yet to be, and having a vision for our life is what keeps us on course.

> Your vision will become clear only when you can look into your own heart. Who looks outside, dreams; who looks inside, awakens.
>
> —CARL JUNG

Do you have a vision for your life? If you don't, it is never too late to create one. Are you willing to look into the depths of your own heart and see who it is you have come here to be? And then are you willing *to do* what it is that you have come here to be? Again, we witness how seamlessly our doing merges with our being when we are willing to consciously enter the mystery of that which is yet to be and follow the path.

A vision of a life worth living will include ongoing opportunities for you to serve others and the world in ways that make the world a better place for all beings and creatures. Living in your true vision will also bring passion and joy to your life that will naturally and effortlessly spill over into the lives of others. When you are living in your vision, you will be led to do work where your God-given talents and skills are utilized and where time seems to pass very quickly. A true vision will always call you to higher ground and cause you to seek to be part of something larger than yourself. Perhaps, more than anything else, having a vision of a life worth living will cause you to grow on an ongoing basis. Your vision as reality will require definite action that may cause a few new "stretch marks." Stretch marks are caused by growth: A person living a vision-led life must be not only open to, but in constant search of, growth. There is no growth at the center of your comfort zone—you already know you have to come to the edge and lean over into the unknown if you want to grow. Living in uncertainty is not the issue—it comes with the territory—however, holding a clear intention for a life worth living, and pursuing it, is. So, the question is: What is your vision for your life? What do you stand for and are you willing to grow into that vision? Begin to use your "Inner I," commingling your mind and heart, and you will see the possibilities of a life you have never known before. Then, pay attention to your intention and follow your vision.

POINTS TO PONDER & PERSONALIZE

* Can you relate to my dog, Mac? Do your best intentions ever get sidelined by the incessant "puppy mind" need for the instant gratification of a diversion? When it does, are you aware of it? I can't count how often, while sitting at the computer, my "puppy mind" will wander off and start making a mess. If I am in the middle of developing a thought or idea, and my mind gets "vapor locked" (my terminology for writer's block), rather than steadfastly keeping my attention on the task at hand, the temptation is to yield to the "pull of the puppy mind" by stopping to check my e-mail or mak-

ing a phone call, and so on. When that happens, if I am mindful, I can actually witness that need for instant gratification pulling me off task, and that is when I will, literally, say out loud, "*Sit* . . . stay, and be here now." Then, after a deep and intentional breath (and sometimes a chuckle), I get back on task. It is quite remarkable the lengths to which we will go to avoid the discipline of delayed gratification that comes with paying attention to the task at hand. How about you? Can you identify any areas in your life where you fail to pay attention to your intentions? By simply becoming the observer of your behavior when it happens, you can teach your mind the command of "Sit . . . stay, and be here now." Try it—you'll be amazed at how well it can work! When your mind is fully "trained," you will be well prepared for your journey into the mystery of that which is yours to unfold.

- When was the last time you headed out the door of your home, jumped into your car, and just started driving in whichever direction your car was pointed with absolutely no destination in mind, going nowhere other than where the road had predetermined it would take you? You probably don't do that too often because usually in your day-to-day life you have a picture in your mind of where you are headed, be it to work, the grocery store, or to grandma's house. Oddly enough, however, when it comes to the long view of where you are headed over a lifetime of seventy, eighty, or ninety years, you seldom have a picture in your mind of where you would like to be at the end of the journey. With a little work, you can learn to live a vision-led life, charting the course of your own destiny.

• What does it mean to "live with a vision"? To have a vision is to simply hold a picture in your mind of a completed idea, knowing that whatever needs to take place to bring it to fruition is now unfolding. The skill comes in learning how to return to the vision when you have momentarily gone unconscious (the attack of the puppy mind) and are drifting. The secret is to hold a picture of yourself as *already* "living the dream" long enough in your mind's eye that you will be drawn toward it every time you are pulled off course. In *The Science of Mind*, Ernest Holmes writes, "What we concentrate, then, is attention. This is done through intention and the willingness to hold thought centered until the form appears." In other words, paying attention to your intention is the practice. Create the most vivid, full-colored, detailed picture in your mind of what your vision looks like *in its completed state* and pay attention to it every day.

• Too often, the course of our lives is altered by what goes on around us on a daily basis. Admiral Omar Nelson Bradley wrote, "We need to learn to set our course by the stars, not by the lights of every passing ship." To me, this means that a person living a vision-led life charts his or her course by using a guidance system that is not affected by the passing parade of life with all of its waves of distraction, and it is not afraid of uncertainty. That guidance system, as discussed in previous chapters, is the Infinite Intelligence within each of us, simply waiting for us to call It forward. Make sure you leave space in your vision for your partnership with Spirit. Making the journey into the mystery of the unknown becomes an exciting adventure when we know we do not travel alone.

MINDFULNESS PRACTICES

Learning how to pay attention to your intention is a process. Learning how to live in your vision before it materializes is an act of faith. Creating and fulfilling your vision of a life worth living is a marriage of intention, attention, faith, and action—in that order. These

Mindfulness Practices will serve in moving you toward the life that awaits you in the mystery of that which you have yet to create.

1. Become the observer of where the energy of your attention is currently being focused. What intention is your attention focused most of the time? Do you have unrealized desires for your life floating around in your heart that you may have been avoiding? If so, are you willing to call them out and make them "conscious" intentions?

   • Before you answer "yes," be certain of one thing: Your *true* intentions are *always* being served, which includes any intention you may hold (even at a very low level of awareness) to stay stuck right where you are in life.

   • The Universe is willing to do Its part—are you? If you are, declare one new intention by writing it down right now while you are thinking about it. Make it your mission to be a conscious observer and pay attention to your intention every day until it becomes ingrained in your mind and your habit energy kicks in. If the "puppy mind" shows up, lovingly tell it to *sit* and stay.

2. For the next few days consider what your vision of
   a life worth living might be. Live in the question,
   "What do I truly want my life in the future to look
   like, and am I willing to follow that vision through
   the uncharted waters of uncertainty?"

   • Pay attention to your feelings, especially those that
     may be causing you extreme *discomfort* or extreme
     excitement. If you sense a feeling of either extreme
     stirring within, it may well be the voice of the In-
     finite One saying, "Okay, it's time to stop drifting
     and chart a course. . . . What have you come here
     to do in my Name? Where are you going with all
     of that Divine Potential I gave you? Let's get on
     with your life!"

   • Realize before you can be pulled by a vision, you
     have to be available. If you listen intently and fear-
     lessly, the vision will be revealed in its own time
     and space. Work at simply being available to your
     own inner guidance system today.

   • Don't concern yourself with the "how." That will
     come after the "where" is firmly seeded. Set your
     compass and trust the process. Infinite Intelligence
     knows how to get you there, even through the wa-
     ters of uncertainty.

3. On your journey there will be times when, regardless of how well focused you are on your intention, things will happen that sidetrack you. Here are three additional practices you can perform that will keep you moving toward the life you desire to live:

- Be gentle with yourself when you fall down (or backslide). The practice is not to beat yourself up, but rather to get back up and continue moving in the direction you previously charted.

- Pace yourself with some form of measurable results, such as a daily journal to log your progress, celebrating certain earmark accomplishments along the way.

- Don't share your goals (vision) with the trolls, meaning those who will try to undermine your success. Do, however, invite a trusted friend, counselor, or mentor to be your faithful cheerleader and lovingly hold you accountable for what you say you are going to do.

- Living in the mystery of life and loving it is simple if you know how: Intention + Attention = Vision + Courage + Faith + Action = A life worth living.

Take a deep breath, smile, and know that you are becoming a master of the art of uncertainty.

14.

REMEMBERING TO REMEMBER
WHO WE ARE, WHERE WE ARE,
AND WHY WE ARE

Mindfulness Makes the Mystery Meaningful

The practice of mindfulness begins in the small, remote cave of your unconscious mind and blossoms with the sunlight of your conscious life, reaching far beyond the people and places you can see.

—EARON DAVIS

From antiquity, spiritual masters have taught that we are on a spiritual journey every moment of our lives. The questions we must fathom for ourselves are these: What is the purpose of this journey and how aware are we that every moment is a spiritual continuum? Mindful living invites us to step into the mystery of the moment, where a deeper understanding of these questions awaits us.

From the perspective of a spiritual journey, it would appear that on the day of birth the soul's essence was instantly squeezed into a very small, dense physical container called a body, and that the individual was instantly labeled according to gender, ethnicity, name, and so on. As we aged, even more labels were acquired until now it seems that we have forgotten who we really are and why we are here. Instead, the focus has become living up to, or in some cases *down to,* the labels that define us in the world. For many of us, however, one day something triggers a remembrance and we begin to recall, if only vaguely, what our purpose on this planet might be. In that moment of awakening, we begin peeling away the labels, and the journey into uncertainty takes on a new significance. As we remember who we really are, we become aware that we *each* have a spiritual purpose. In her book *Unlimited Visibility,* Stephanie Sorensen writes, "Even though it may seem like it, it isn't that some people have a specific purpose in life while the rest of us are simply aimless extras. We all play an integral part in the Divine Picture of Creation." Mindful living is the art and practice of *remembering to remember* the role we play—who we are, where we are, and *why* we are on this journey. As we venture into the mystery of it all with mindfulness, our journey takes us inward where we plumb the depths of Self, in addition to our outward exploration of our world. As we experience the journey in both directions, we will increasingly discover more of who we really are . . . and who we are not.

> Our primordial purpose is to respond to the impulsion from within to solve the mystery of our individual existence, to find the authentic Self that is, has been and ever shall be.
>
> —MICHAEL BERNARD BECKWITH

Mindful living is a lifestyle. It's a way of consciously walking a sacred earth experience, incorporating purpose and an awareness of Divine Presence in all that we say, think, and do on our journey in this lifetime. Discovering the authentic Self will never have a point of arrival because the Self we seek is Infinite. Talk about uncertainty! But the deeper we go on the quest, the more peace we shall find as we discover more of who we truly are. This quest, if we are to honor the calling, will require us to continue to come to the edge of uncertainty time and time again. This doesn't mean every few years, or even in those times when we may experience those unavoidable life-changing events; it means *every day* of our lives. It is only in the mystery of that which is yet to be that we shall find the authentic Self we have each come here to ultimately be.

As we awaken to our soul's purpose, we inherently know that it is found in our daily experience. In his book *The Living Universe*, Duane Elgin describes our journey into the mystery of uncertainty this way: "We are spiritual beings having a bodily experience. Our bodies are biodegradable vehicles for acquiring soul-growing experiences. Every experience plants its feeling-knowing resonance in our soul." In other words, our reason for existing is right in front of us, in the mystery of every moment of every day. The mystery really does lie in every present moment because no one knows what it shall bring. However, the challenge for most of us is that our minds are often somewhere *other* than in the present moment.

The day we were born, life became a linear process where we learned *doing* was very important and *time* became a commodity. This is when we began to get "spiritual amnesia," and began forgetting who we really are. We were taught how to project ourselves into the future so we might one day create a life of meaning and purpose by accomplishing one goal after another, moving from one grade to the next, getting through school, acquiring a job, finding a partner, creating a home, and so on—essentially acquiring even more labels as we went along. Indeed, we learned how to *do* life very well on this linear pathway and, in the process, most of us forgot how to *be*. Some say time is moving so fast that having a spiritual experience is very challenging; there's so much to do. In actuality, time is standing still because it's always *now*—it is *we* who are moving so quickly through time. Living mindfully can slow us down and bring us consciously and intentionally into the mystery of the present moment, which is where we find our spiritual experience *waiting for us* to open to Its greatest gift: The peace that passes all understanding.

WITH MINDFULNESS LIFE BECOMES SEAMLESS

> Can you tell me where "this" moment ends and the "next" begins? Where the subject ends and the object begins? Where the observer ends and the observed begins? Where you end and the world begins? Where is this dividing line?
>
> —Dr. John Astin

Right now, if you intentionally take a deep breath, and focus on that breath, you will discover that your mind and your body are in the same place at the same time.

The irony is, our body can't be any place other than in the present moment. But far too often, our mind is elsewhere. Mindfulness is the practice of calling the thinking mind back to where the body is so that the two become *as one* in the present moment. As you incorporate awareness of Infinite Presence in the moment, *doing* becomes seamlessly infused with *being* as *the activity at hand*. In *The Science of Mind*, Ernest Holmes writes, "A new light is coming into the world. We are on the borderland of a new experience. The veil between Spirit and matter is very thin. The invisible passes into visibility through our faith in it." At this level of mindful living, the perceived dividing line between doing and being, matter and Divine essence, and you and your soul Self, begins to slowly blur and, ultimately, dissolve. This is when every action becomes a spiritual experience, be it driving the car, mowing the lawn, changing the baby's diaper, selling real estate, performing brain surgery, or making love to your significant other. As you deepen your consciousness to fully embody the practice of mindful living, all of life becomes a sacred continuum. We might say that, in the mystery of the present moment, there are no dividing lines—there is only the One, in which we all live, move, and have our being.

BEING PRESENT WITH
NONJUDGMENT OPENS THE
PORTAL TO ONENESS

To further expand on what this experience of oneness feels like, I share a passage from my book *The Art of Being: 101 Ways to Practice Purpose in Your Life*: "What I have also discovered is that when that sense of seamless oneness does happen, there are always two specific points of awareness accompanying it: One, I notice that I am 'being' in the now moment. Regardless of what is going on, where I am, whom I am with, or what it looks like, I realize I am 100 percent present there, spiritually, mentally, and physically; my mind is not off, wandering around in the past or the future. Two, I have an overwhelming awareness that I am operating in a 'nonjudgment' mode where the energy of unconditional love goes before me, filling in all the gaps and spaces between myself and the world and everyone in it, where my otherwise judgmental little self might be slapping labels all over my every experience, creating a sense of 'two-ness' or separation, rather than oneness." My point is that mindfulness in the mystery of the moment is the portal to our oneness with Life. In other words, our bliss is right in front of our noses 24/7.

MINDFUL LIVING REMINDS
US OF OUR BLESSINGS

> When we have a toothache, we know that not hav-
> ing a toothache is happiness. But later, when we
> don't have a toothache, we don't treasure our non-
> toothache. Practicing mindfulness helps us learn to
> appreciate the well-being that is already there.
>
> —THICH NHAT HANH

As we master the art of uncertainty, we learn the value
and meaning of being present because in every "Now"
moment there lies a silent blessing we might have otherwise overlooked. Isn't it amazing how often we don't
take time to truly appreciate something until it is gone?
We get complacent and slip into a "take life for granted"
mode; in other words, we get comfortable with perceived
"certainties." This happens many times in relationships,
and often with our material status, but even more so
with our physical well-being. Consider some of the "non-
problems" you have in your life *at this moment*. When was
the last time you appreciated your heart and liver for the
great job they do at keeping you healthy and alive? What
about the roof over your head? Do you ever take your
body and home for granted? How about the relationships

you have with your partner, family, and friends that give deep meaning to your existence? Would this be a good day to call someone you love and tell them so? The wisdom found in the art of uncertainty affirms that every sacred second is a gift and that mindfulness can help us *remember* to remember to come back to the present and appreciate the blessings of the moment, taking nothing for granted. Don't wait until you have a toothache to be appreciative of how good a "non-toothache" feels. Don't wait until your coworker has gone home to say, "Good job." Don't wait until a loved one is no longer there to say, "I love you." Don't wait until you have "time" to be mindful. With mindfulness, we will remember that every moment *is* the time.

MINDFUL BREATHING ANCHORS US WHEN LIFE BECOMES TURBULENT

> Only let the moving waters calm down, and the sun and moon will be reflected on the surface of your being.
>
> —RUMI

Often, when I am presenting a lecture or workshop, I will pause and say to everyone in attendance, "How are you breathing right now—and by that I don't just mean, in and out." They will chuckle, smile, and then realize that they really were not breathing all that deeply. Then, I will invite them to take a deep, intentional breath and witness the difference it makes in bringing them into the present moment. I now invite you to do the same thing— go to your breath and witness how you are breathing— then take an intentionally deep breath and feel the difference. When we breathe deeply, intentionally, and mindfully, it anchors us in our bodies. My goal is to get people to be present enough *in* their body to fully *be* wherever they are, in spirit, mind, and body. When we first become conscious of our breathing, we may be taken aback by how shallow or rapid it is at any given moment, especially those times when we are under stress or our minds are churning with everyday concerns. It's difficult to be present in the Presence when daily life is full of distractions. However, the waters of a turbulent mind will never reflect the light Rumi refers to, which is a metaphor for Infinite Presence. Learning how to breathe consciously is an essential practice for mindful living because it can bring us back to the mystery of the present moment, which is where Life is waiting for us to fully engage. Mindful breathing is a key element in being present with "what is." Our minds are always moving here and there—most often lingering in either the happenings of the past, be they ten minutes or ten years ago, or the concerns of the future, be they ten minutes or ten years from now. In either case, we have no power there, so we would be much better served by fully being where our true point of power lies: In the mystery of the present moment, where anything is possible. The question is, what can we do to calm the waters in the present moment?

LISTEN MINDFULLY TO THE SILENCE BETWEEN BREATHS

> Breathing in, I calm my body.
> Breathing out, I smile.
> Dwelling in the present moment
> I know this is a wonderful moment.
>
> —THICH NHAT HANH

For many of us, the waters of our daily life are anything but calm because we don't create conscious space for intentional breathing or silence as part of our daily experience. When we stop to consider it, breathing is the most life-essential thing we do, and it is *always* a present-moment experience. However, seldom are we consciously aware that we are breathing. When we pause and breathe consciously, we open the portal to the Presence and enter a sacred silence where the waters are always calm.

Occasionally, early in the morning before I do my daily meditation, I go to my piano and sit quietly. With my eyes closed, I gently place my fingers on the keys and, when inspired, begin to slowly play only single notes with no song in mind, just allowing my fingers to go where they are led to go. For me, this is also an exercise in living in the uncertainty of what the next key I press shall be, and it is an appropriate metaphor for how we can approach every minute of the day when we are mindful in and of the moment. As a form of mindfulness practice, after each note I play, I mindfully draw in a deep breath and, while slowly releasing that breath, I listen to the silence that arises between each note played as it fades. From a musician's perspective, the space between the notes is as important as the notes themselves. Without the silence (or gap) between the notes, there would be no music. Instead, it would be one long, continuous run-on noise that becomes meaningless. Likewise, the silent spaces between our breaths and thoughts are equally as important because the Infinite is ever waiting for us to create that sacred opening in the present moment into which It may flow. Again, the mystery of the moment invites us to breathe into it, merge with that which is yet to be, and witness the creative process as it unfolds. The good news is that you don't need a piano to create that sacred space. In the Mindfulness Practices at the end of this chapter I will offer you a breathing technique that will help you calm the waters of a turbulent mind.

> By having a reverence for life, we enter into a spiritual relation with the world. By practicing reverence for life we become good, deep, and alive.
>
> —ALBERT SCHWEITZER

Living mindfully with reverence is remembering to remember that we live in a spiritual universe wherein everyone and everything is interconnected in a sacred web of oneness. Reverence is seeing through all appearances: The shell, the form, and the effect or condition, and then honoring the sacred at the center or all that is. When we activate reverence in our life, everything we do becomes a sacred act: Every relationship becomes another opportunity to see the face of the Beloved; every meal we eat becomes another way to affirm our unity with the Source from whence that meal came. In short, life becomes our pathway to being on purpose. Our purpose is to be the place where, metaphorically, heaven touches earth. In short, mindful living blesses each of us and our world. Living mindfully makes every relationship sacred, every challenge on our pathway a stepping stone rather than a stumbling block, and every day an opportunity to live with a sense of awe, meaning, and purpose. The journey of our soul really is the journey of a lifetime, and it's a journey we get to take whether we are aware or not. Mindful living brings awareness to the journey and frees us from the limitation of the labels that have defined us from the day we were born. With this in mind, as we continue our sojourn into the mystery of uncertainty, let us "remember to remember" that the best is yet to be.

POINTS TO PONDER & PERSONALIZE

- Can you relate to the idea that your presence on the planet is not by mistake—that you are here "on purpose," and that your body serves as the perfect vessel by means of which you acquire soul-growing experiences? If so, can you see how mindfulness will help you be more fully present with every experience you have, drawing maximum value and meaning from it? Does this awareness alleviate any fear or concerns regarding what lies ahead on the pathway of uncertainty? Knowing your life is on purpose will make the mystery of that which is yet to be an exciting journey.

- As you begin to practice mindfulness in every area of your life, notice also how time appears to slow down in those moments. As you focus on the present moment, your experience of it will intensify because you are drawing nearer to the Source. This is when the veil between form and the formless begins to disappear and life becomes a seamless flow of energy. This experience alone is part of the mystery of life you have come here to explore.

- There is no area of your life where mindful living will not benefit your well-being . . . and your world. Your physical body and the body of your affairs literally vibrate at a higher frequency when you are mindful of the Infinite Presence in the moment. When you are guided to eat your meals mindfully, remembering the Source from whence it comes, food becomes a blessing to your body temple and you make wiser choices regarding what you put into your body. Your relationships thrive when you are mindful of the presence of the Beloved because reverence and loving-kindness becomes the practice with those with whom you interact. Likewise, at the workplace, mindful living blesses all of those with whom you work or serve. When you are aware of the Presence, every transaction becomes a sacred act, and every product, customer, and employee is blessed by your "remembering to remember." Lastly, when you enter into each day remembering that abundance is the natural out-picturing of one who lives mindfully aware of his or her connection and unity with the Source, you will tend to be more generous with your material good.

- All the aforementioned are beneficent things to remember as we travel the pathway of uncertainty. It is much easier to live in the mystery of life and love it when we stay connected to the Source in every moment. Mindfulness, coupled with reverence, is the practice that connects us.

- May your journey be a conscious one where the intention of your soul intersects with the intention of your human nature on a daily basis, bringing your Being into alignment with your *doing* every moment of your life; you deserve it and so does your world.

MINDFULNESS PRACTICES

Ultimately, every moment is the entry point into the mystery of uncertainty. No one knows what lies beyond the next breath, so why not take that breath mindfully? In doing so, we bring the power of Presence into the present. These Mindfulness Practices will assist you in remembering to remember who you really are, regardless of where you are. When coming to the edge of uncertainty, being mindful is a wise thing to be and practice.

1. This is a mindfulness practice using a silent mantra coupled with a breathing exercise:
   - On a *slow* in-breath (focusing solely on the breath), silently affirm "God is," or "Life is" (in other words, use whatever name for the nameless One that most resonates with you), then gently hold that breath for approximately six seconds while mindfully observing the space created by non-breathing. Then on a *slow* out-breath silently affirm, "I am."
   - Repeat the cycle in a rhythm for ten minutes (longer, if possible) silently affirming "God is . . . I am" and notice how a sense of inner peace rises

in the field of your awareness and the waters are calmed.

2. When you eat your next meal, do so as a mindfulness practice.

   - As you *slowly* chew your food consider the idea that you are not just eating fruit, lettuce, or a piece of bread, you are eating the energy of the Sun, the rain, and even the farmer who brought the crops to harvest.

   - Put a single piece of fruit in your mouth and truly experience the taste, texture, and essence of that fruit. Allow your taste buds to report to you the experience they are having. Pay attention to nothing other than what is going on in your mouth in that moment. Does this experience enliven your sense of connectedness to the Source?

3. Instead of turning on your television tonight, go outside, sit down (or lie down if possible), and gaze at the moon or a bright star.

   - As you soften your gaze, focus on your breathing and imagine the Infinite Intelligence at work in that holy instant, holding the entire universe in place in divine order and balance. Enjoy the awe of that realization and be with your breath.

- Then, gently close your eyes and turn within and imagine the same Infinite Intelligence maintaining your body with the same orderliness and balance—beating your heart, converting the food you had for dinner into the energy of skin, hair, organs, and so on. Enjoy the awe of that realization as well, realizing you are one with the universe.

The next time you come to the edge of uncertainty, through either inspiration or desperation, remember these Mindfulness Practices and take time to do them. You will feel the power of Presence with you, then and there. Mindfulness does, indeed, make the mystery meaningful, yes?

CONCLUSION

The Journey to the Place We Never Really Left

❧

People travel to wonder at the height of mountains,
at the huge waves of the sea, at the long courses of
rivers, at the vast compass of the ocean, at the circular motion of the stars . . . and they pass by themselves without wondering.

—St. Augustine

We have discussed and explored the use of tools, techniques, and Mindfulness Practices that make living in the mystery of that which is yet to be not just manageable, but an adventure to look forward to. However, the deepest mystery, and perhaps the one for which there will never be an answer that will completely satisfy the itch of the intellect, is the miracle of Life itself. In his book *The Living Universe*, Duane Elgin writes, "American Indian lore speaks of three miracles. The first miracle is that anything exists at all. The second miracle is that living things exist. The third miracle is that living things exist that know they exist. As human beings conscious of ourselves, we represent the third miracle." In the normal course of our daily life, these three miracles are all mysteries we seldom take time to contemplate, if ever. However, when we are fully conscious, it is the mystery of the third miracle of self-awareness that allows us to gaze directly into the face of the "Beloved" each time we look into a mirror. We expend much of our time and energy navigating over, under, around, and through the uncertainties of everyday life, relating to the events, conditions, and circumstances that come with the territory of living in a human skin. The intent of this book has been to help us better learn how to live on the edge of uncertainty, not just to endure it, but to love it! That alone will lead us to a rewarding life. However, as they say in the TV infomercials, "But wait! . . . there's more." If we fail to apply the core concepts of this book to the largest mystery of all, the miracle of Life, we miss the deeper meaning of our journey altogether.

> If we could see the miracle of a single flower clearly,
> our whole life would change.
>
> —BUDDHA

The idea that we can be conscious of ourselves as human beings has profound implications. It means that we can become observers of the miracle of our own minds at work. It also means, once again, that we can consciously experience that mystical point in space and time when and where our doing merges with our Being. Stop right now, take a deep intentional breath, and then take a peek into your own mind. Simply witness *yourself*, observe *yourself*. When was the last time you paused to do this? Watch your thinking mind process your thoughts, and the ideas being presented here, as you read these words. The fact that when we choose to be fully present in the mystery of the moment, we can be the observer of our own minds means that there is more to us than meets the eye, or the brain—*who is it* that is doing the observing? This is the moment when the human self and the sacred Self commingle as one, and it is also the miracle of all miracles; that is, that in any given moment we can consciously witness the merging of the human with the Divine realizing, as Ernest Holmes wrote, "What we are looking for, we are looking with."

This is the mystical moment when we know we have fully entered the mystery of life at a level where uncertainty of anything ceases to exist. The idea of certainty and uncertainty is a human invention. If humankind did not exist, certainty and uncertainty wouldn't exist, either, because both are a human concern. The Universe, which is Infinite Intelligence, just Is, and It has been operating in its Divine "Is-ness" flawlessly for fourteen billion years and it continues to evolve Itself, expanding at the speed of Light, with no apparent attachment to where it is going or what its future may or may not be. Because uncertainty is our invention, it is we who give meaning and power to it and, therefore, we can revoke that power. As we deepen our awareness of our oneness with this expanding Life Force, uncertainty will cease holding us hostage to what lies ahead in the mystery of that which is yet to be. Then, coming to the edge of the unknown becomes a natural part of our journey that will happen repeatedly, with grace and ease. This does not mean the mystery of that which is yet to be will cease—it simply means we have become one *with it* as it unfolds.

> And the end of all our exploring will be to arrive where we started and know the place for the first time.
>
> —T. S. ELIOT

Life, itself, is the ultimate mystery. It is a miracle that we shall never fully understand, nor should we try: We appear on the planet one day, coming from the apparent ethers of absolute nothingness, entering Earth School with many questions and no answers. As we grow and evolve, we spend the balance of our time on the journey as soul beings learning how to navigate through the human condition, gathering the necessary information to create a life worth living through curiosity, inquisitiveness, and experiences motivated by either desperation or inspiration. As we awaken to our true nature, we aspire to create experiences that offer purpose and meaning for the journey. Then one day, when it is our time, we depart once again, back into the apparent ethers of nothingness from which we came. What is not miraculous *and* mysterious about that? It is what we do *with* the miracle and the mystery between the coming and the going that matters. Another way to say it might be: The most precious gift we have ever been given by the Infinite One is the miracle of Life, itself; what we choose to do with this Life is our gift back to the Giver.

It is with deep respect and appreciation that I thank you for sharing sacred space with me on this most wondrous journey to the place we never really left—our oneness with Infinite Presence. As you continue your journey into the mystery of that which is yet to be, may you know that who you are, and what you do with who you are, matters. When you draw your final breath on this planet, may you know it is a better place than it was when you arrived because you were here. Most of all, may you always come to the edge of your uncertainties and lean over, knowing you were born to soar.

Move and the way will open.

—ZEN PROVERB

Peace,
Dennis Merritt Jones
www.DennisMerrittJones.com

Recommended Reading

Astin, John. *Too Intimate for Words*. Santa Cruz: Integrative Arts, 2005.

————. *This Is Always Enough*. United Kingdom: Non-Duality press, 2007.

Bach, Richard. *Illusions*. Delacorte Press, 1977.

Barks, Coleman. *The Essential Rumi*. New York: Quality Paperback Book Club, 1995.

Beckwith, Michael Bernard. *Spiritual Liberation*. New York: Atria Books, 2009.

Butterworth, Eric. *Spiritual Economics*. Unity Village, MO: Unity School of Christianity, 1983.

Carter-Scott, Cherie. *If Life Is a Game, These Are the Rules*. New York: Broadway Books, 1998.

Chodron, Pema. *When Things Fall Apart*. Boston: Shambhala, 1995.

Chopra, Deepak. *The Seven Spiritual Laws of Success*. New York: Amber-Allen, 1994.

Elgin, Duane. *The Living Universe.* San Francisco, CA: Berrett-Koehier, 2009.

De Mellow, Anthony. *Awareness.* New York: Doubleday, 1990.

_____. *The Way to Love.* New York: Doubleday, 1991.

Ferrucci, Piero. *The Power of Kindness.* New York: Tarcher/Penguin, 2006.

Gibran, Kahlil. *The Prophet.* New York: Alfred Knopf, 1977.

Goldsmith, Barton. *100 Ways to Boost Your Self-Confidence.* New Jersey: Career Press, 2011.

Hanh, Thich Nhat. *The Heart of the Buddha's Teaching.* New York: Broadway Books, 1998.

Hendricks, Gay. *The Big Leap.* New York: HarperCollins, 2008.

Holmes, Ernest. *The Science of Mind.* New York: G. P. Putnam's Sons, 1938.

_____. *This Thing Called You.* New York: Tarcher/Penguin, 2004.

Jampolsky, Gerald. *Love Is Letting Go of Fear.* Berkeley, CA: Celestial Arts, 1979.

Jones, Dennis Merritt. *The Art of Being: 101 Ways to Practice Purpose in Your Life.* New York: Tarcher/Penguin, 2008.

_____. *How to Speak Science of Mind.* Camarillo, CA: DeVorss, 2010.

Kabat-Zinn, Jon. *Wherever You Go, There You Are.* New York: Hyperion, 1994.

Kornfield, Jack. *After the Ecstasy, the Laundry.* New York: Bantam Books, 2000.

_____. *The Art of Forgiveness, Lovingkindness and Peace.* New York: Bantam Books, 2002.

_____. *The Wise Heart.* New York: Bantam Dell, 2008.

Morrissey, Mary Manin. *Building Your Field of Dreams.* New York: Bantam Books, 1996.

————. *No Less than Greatness*. New York: Bantam Books, 2001.

Muktananda, Swami. *Where Are You Going?* South Fallsburg, NY: SYDA Foundation, 1994.

Muller, Wayne. *How, Then, Shall We Live?* New York: Bantam Books, 1996.

Pauch, Randy. *The Last Lecture*. New York: Hyperion, 2008.

Prakashananda, Swami. *Don't Think of a Monkey*. Freemont, CA: Sarasvati Productions, 1994.

Ruiz, Don Miguel. *The Four Agreements*. San Rafael, CA: Amber-Allen, 1997.

Sorensen, Stephanie. *Unlimited Visibility*. Camarillo, CA: DeVorss, 1996.

————. *The Sacred Continuum*. Camarillo, CA: DeVorss, 2000.

Starcke, Walter. *It's All God*. Boerne, TX: The Guadalupe Press, 1998.

Tolle, Eckhart. *The Power of Now*. Navato, CA: New World, 1999.

————. *A New Earth*. New York: Dutton, 2005.

Zukav, Gary. *The Seat of the Soul*. New York: Fireside, 1989.

————. *Soul to Soul*. New York: Free Press, 2007.

————. *Spiritual Partnership*. New York: Harper One, 2010.

Zukav, Gary, and Linda Francis. *The Heart of the Soul*. New York: Simon & Schuster, 2001.

Acknowledgments

It is with great respect and gratitude that I acknowledge those who have supported me in bringing this book to fruition: To my wife, business partner, and best friend, Diane, for graciously allowing me the time and space in our relationship to honor the Divine Nudge when this book was ready to be given birth. To my dog, Mac, for his vigilance in lying under my desk, keeping my feet warm, my heart open, and my mind present in the moment. To my literary agent, Lynn Garrett, for coaching (and coddling) me through the process of fine-tuning a compelling book proposal. To my publisher, Joel Fotinos, at Tarcher/Penguin, for seeing the potential in this book and then inviting me to come to the edge of my own uncertainties by writing it. To my friend Gary Peattie, who throughout the years has not only encouraged me as a writer, but has modeled what authentic loving-kindness looks like.

To my longtime friend and associate Stephanie Sorensen, for her talent and discerning eye in doing the preliminary edit. To my two longtime prayer partners Sue Rubin and Patrick Cameron, for continually knowing the truth about me in those moments when I have forgotten who I really am. Their prayer support helped make this book a reality. To my parents, Russell and Evelyn Jones, and all members of the Great Generation who were able to create lives worth living for themselves and their families by embracing the challenges and uncertainties of their time. They have modeled and proven that the possibilities for an abundant and good life lie in the mystery of the unknown. To my friends and peers in the global New Thought spiritual community, especially those affiliated with the Centers for Spiritual Living located throughout the United States, Canada, and other parts of the world. To the many great minds that I quote throughout this book. To Ernest Holmes and the other spiritual giants upon whose shoulders I stand. Lastly, to the Divine One, who is the real creator of this book. With humility and boundless love, I say thank you all.

About the Author

Throughout his lifetime, Dennis Merritt Jones has been on a quest to inspire and lift people to a higher expression of life. His personal vision is to guide people to their purpose, knowing that when people fully awaken to who they are and why they are on the planet, they naturally begin to share their gift with humankind and, in the process, create an enriching life for themselves and the world around them.

Dennis is the author of the award-winning book *The Art of Being: 101 Ways to Practice Purpose in Your Life*, released by Tarcher/Penguin, and *How to Speak Science of Mind*.

Dennis believes we each have the capacity and, ultimately, the responsibility to contribute something positive to this world, leaving it a better place than it was when we arrived—concepts that are reflected in his writings. He uses his understanding of universal principles to draw upon wisdom from both Eastern and Western philosophies. Dennis believes that there is a new consciousness of unity, cooperation, and reverence rising in humankind, where the value of all life is considered sacred. He believes this consciousness of unity, cooperation, and reverence for life and the planet will be one of the most significant influences upon society as we approach the challenges and uncertainties of twenty-first-century living.

Dennis was the founder and spiritual director of the Center for Spiritual Living in Simi Valley, California, for twenty-three years. He retired from the pulpit in 2008 to take his message to the world by means of his books, spiritual mentoring, keynote speaking, consulting, and seminars.

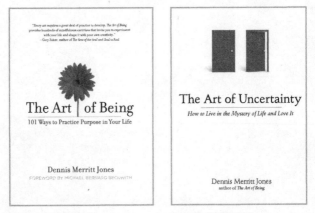

Dennis brings his personal vision of "guiding people to purpose" to the world through his books, keynote speaking, workshops, retreats, consulting, and mentoring. He may be reached through his website:

www.DennisMerrittJones.com